When Huai Flowers Bloom

When Huai Flowers Bloom

槐花

Stories of the
Cultural Revolution

Shu Jiang Lu

STATE UNIVERSITY OF NEW YORK PRESS

Published by
State University of New York Press, Albany

© 2007 State University of New York

All rights reserved

Printed in the United States of America

For information, contact
State University of New York Press, Albany, NY
www.sunypress.edu

Production by Marilyn P. Semerad
Marketing by Susan M. Petrie

Library of Congress Cataloging in Publication Data

Lu, Shu Jiang.
When Huai flowers bloom : stories of the Cultural Revolution / Shu Jiang Lu.
    p. cm.
Includes Bibliographical references.
ISBN 978-0-7914-7231-6 (alk. paper)
    1. China—History—Cultural Revolution, 1966–1976—Personal narratives.
I. Title. II. Title: Stories of the Cultural Revolution.

DS778.7.L84 2007
951.05'6—dc22

                                                          2006101367

10 9 8 7 6 5 4 3 2 1

To my father
For everything you have taught me

Contents

Acknowledgments   *ix*

Prologue   *xi*

1. I Heard a Bird Singing   *1*

2. The Fragrance of Huai Flowers   *23*

3. Pear Flower Alley   *41*

4. Jade Rabbit   *53*

5. The Voices of the Winds   *63*

6. The Song of the Golden Phoenix   *81*

7. Fairyland   *99*

8. The Girl under the Red Flag   *111*

9. A World of Rain   *127*

10. The Winter Solstice   *143*

11. Sunset   *161*

12. Beyond Darkness   *175*

Epilogue   *189*

Acknowledgments

I wish to express my profound gratitude and deepest appreciation to the following people:

To SUNY Press for its trust, to Acquisitions Editor Nancy Ellegate for her belief in the book, to Editorial Assistant Allison Lee, Publicist Susan Petrie, and Director of Production Marilyn Semerad, for their hard work, and also to David Lee Prout for his deft and perceptive editorial touch;

To my mentor and dear friend, Elizabeth Hodges, for her care, grace, and invaluable assistance and guidance every step of the way;

To my professors in Canada for their wisdom, patience, and generosity;

To my friends and colleagues at University of Pittsburgh at Greensburg for their kindness and support; I am particularly indebted to Rich Blevins, Martha Koehler, Lori Jakiela and Judy Vollmer whose enthusiasm in this project and steady encouragement keep me going and whose insightful comments and suggestions help me walk more deeply into the narrative;

To the editor of *Facets*, an online literary magazine in which an early draft of the last chapter appeared;

To all my students who have shared their stories with me and have inspired me to write mine;

To my mother, my sisters, and brother in China for their love and faith in me;

To my dearest husband and best friend, Xiaogang Guo, and my beautiful daughter, Anying Guo, for being a constant source of strength and inspiration;

Finally, in memory, to my father, who taught me how telling and listening to stories can help us endure the most difficult times and dream the most beautiful dreams. For this and much more, I am forever grateful.

Prologue

Once upon a time, there is a mountain.

In the mountain, there is a temple.

In the temple, there is an old monk who lives with a young monk.

One day, the old monk tells the young monk a story.

He starts: "Once upon a time, there is a mountain, and in the mountain, there is a temple, and in the temple, there is a monk who lives with a young monk. One day the old monk tells the young monk a story. He says: 'Once upon a time . . .'"

So the telling continues, never ending. Like a bird, it wings its way through the thickest forest of the mountain, over its valley and up to its top. As darkness falls, it perches quietly on the clear full moon hanging over the edge of the vast dark blue skyline. Every now and then, large pieces of clouds scud over the moon, shredding it into strips that seem to be falling into the darkness below. But each time the moon emerges, full as ever, so does the bird, waiting in the quiet darkness for the break of the dawn when it will fly, sing, and tell stories, for another day.

And another, another, and another. It never ends.

槐花 1

I Heard a Bird Singing

Once upon a time, there was a Dragon King who lived on the top of a big mountain in a palace built with golden bricks and covered with silver shingles. The King, dressed in a sparkling yellow dragon robe and sitting high above on his dragon throne, issued his royal commands to his subjects. One day, the King ordered that trees be planted around the palace. And they must be the same kind with the same shape and same color. The King's wish was immediately fulfilled. Trees of the same bright red color and the same heart-shaped leaves were planted around the palace. The King, looking down from the top of the mountain, was pleased with what he saw and further demanded, "You are all my subjects." His thunderous voice echoed through the hill and valley. "You must always strive to maintain your color, mind you, because that is the color of loyalty, your loyalty to me, your King. You must not let the color fade; you must not change the shape. Keep still and quiet unless I tell you otherwise." All the trees cringed. Awed and silenced by those words, they offered their leaves— their hearts—for the King to play with, to tear, or to burn, at the mercy of his boundless power.

As days went by, some of the younger trees became more and more restless and resentful. "Our eyes are so burned all day by this red color," they burst out one day, "that our vision is all but a blur now; our sight is trapped in the forest and we can hardly see a meter away. Our voices have

1

been silenced for so long that our throats are growing rusty and our words caged within like dead birds." Adult trees nervously turned to these grumbling youngsters, hushing and shushing them. Their trunks were shivering with panic and their voices shaking with fear. "What do you need your voice for? You should be grateful just to be alive. Understand? You'd better watch out your mouth, or you will bring disasters to your families and yourselves. The King is on the top of the mountain. He knows everything about us. So you'd better shut your mouths, now and forever."

That was the warning I grew up on, the warning that was passed on to us from our parents' generation who had learned through endless class struggles and political movements how words—a slip of the tongue or a single sentence spoken ten years earlier—could turn one into an enemy of the state and wipe out one's existence.

"You know how your father escaped being smeared as a rightist in the 1957 Anti-Rightist Movement?" My mother often reminded us. "He didn't say anything during those arranged study sessions and meetings. If he had, this family wouldn't be here, I tell you. We would be plowing fields and planting rice in some remote village. We would grow old and die there. So would you."

And she was right. In the chilly early spring of 1957, the Party called for all intellectuals, Party members and nonmembers alike, to voice their views to help the Party improve itself. Not knowing that this was a trap set up by the Party and its Great Leader to identify and capture any potential enemies, or—to use Chairman Mao's own words—to "lure snakes out of their lairs," many authors, poets, artists, researchers, and professors spoke their minds freely. As a result, they were labeled as anti-Party rightists and were uprooted from cities and forced into exile in rural areas and labor reform farms. If my father had done the same, he would have had his city residential permit revoked like many others and been sent to a labor farm or back to his home village. If my mother chose not to divorce him, like many other wives were forced to do—for their children's sake—she would have been expelled from the city along with her husband. My second sister, my brother, and I would have been born peasants.

The lesson was learned by all. Watch your mouth. Say the right things. Follow the crowd. Parrot the words. Grown-ups warned themselves, each other, and their children. Remember, the sun is always shining, the east is always red, and the Party is forever great. To survive was to say what everyone else said and be able to show that you were the same as everyone else. Think as stipulated by our Great Leader and his Party, cast away all doubts, and keep to the slogans. Learn to lie, to wear a mask, and to extinguish your voice or else hide it deep at the bottom of your heart. Words could get you into trouble and disaster always came from your mouth.

Remember, remember.

And yet . . .

I didn't want to remember. I tried to break the imposed silence by telling stories, stories I heard from my grandmother and my father and later learned on my own. I listened to my voice flapping its wings over the silent wall into an overcast sky. Like a bird, once it has flown from its cage, it will not want to fly back into it again.

When at the age of twenty-one, my mother had her first child, my oldest sister, in the spring of 1954, my grandma moved from Bengbu, an industrial city in the north of Anhui Province, to Hefei, the provincial capital where my family lived, to help take care of her first grandchild, and three more afterward. She became a migrating bird, flying back and forth between Bengbu and Hefei. Each time she came, she had to stay longer and longer, as my parents had to leave us more and more frequently. My mother, working full time as a librarian, was obligated to go to the countryside at least once a month to assist peasants with political movements. My father, an author and also a Party member, had to spend a good six to eight months in the distant rural areas, working as a Party secretary in different communes and writing at the same time.

The void left by my parents was filled by my grandma under whose wings we all huddled, feeling her soft blue cotton dajing shirt, smelling the fragrance of her hair oil, and listening to her mellow voice from which folk tales, opera romances, and ghost stories trickled like a clear-water creek. The heat and humidity of summers retreated as we sat on our cool bamboo bed under the dark blue starry sky. My grandmother, sitting right beside our bed, waved a big palm fan back and forth to chase away ferocious mosquitoes that otherwise would have eaten us alive. As the fan danced with a steady rhythm, it turned into a magic wand with whose help we flew to the quiet and vast Moon Palace where we would meet the beautiful Moon Lady (Chang-O) who offered us a jar of sweet osmanthus wine and invited us to dance with her. We would follow Jade Rabbit, gliding over the surface of the moon, trying to catch a floating cloud. From the moon palace, we would then fly toward the Silver River (the Milky Way) where we joined the Weaving Fairy (Vega) on one side and then the Buffalo Boy (Altair) on the other.

"Did you see those two smaller stars on each side of the Altair?" my grandma would sigh. "They are the Weaving Fairy and Buffalo Boy's children—a boy and a girl. When the Weaving Fairy fell in love with Buffalo Boy, she sneaked out of the Heavenly Palace and married him. They lived a happy and peaceful life on earth, the Buffalo Boy plowing in the field and the Fairy weaving cloth at home. But the Fairy's mother, the Western Celestial Queen, had her snatched back to the palace and forbade her to return to earth. The Buffalo Boy, with the help of a magic water buffalo, flew all the way to the Heavenly Palace, carrying their children on a shoulder pole, one on each side. When he was near the entrance of the palace, the Queen pulled out her hair pin and scratched a Silver River in the sky that forever separated the Buffalo Boy and the Weaving Fairy. But every year, on the seventh day in the seventh month of each lunar year, magpies with red, orange, blue, silver, and golden feathers gather from all corners of China to build a bridge across the Silver River so that the Weaving Fairy and the Buffalo Boy can be together for that day."

The icy chill of the roaring north wind subsided as we curled up inside our cotton quilt, watching different dramas unfold from behind my grandmother's magical curtain of words. We followed Liniang to the Peony Pavilion where she secretly became engaged to her lover against her father's wishes. We followed the route of the Princess of White Snake to the Broken Bridge over the West Lake in the city of Hang Zhou, an earthly paradise, where she fell in love with a handsome and kind-hearted scholar and fought to the death for their love against an evil monk. Then we listened to the wrongly accused Dou O, her voice of protest echoing through the heavens, declaring that on the day she was to be beheaded, the river would turn red and there would be a snow storm in June (the Sixth Month according to the lunar calendar). Everything happened exactly as she predicted. The power of her words finally carried out vengeance for the injustice done to her.

After each story, my grandma never forgot to add, "What I have told you, do not tell to anyone else, hear me? Those are all old stories. Don't tell them outside the house. Remember."

We all nodded, knowing well that the word "old," as in the old society, always carried with it a derogatory connotation. The Party and its Leader called on people to build a shining brand-new society and urged them to transform themselves into new people with pure revolutionary minds and spirits. These stories about fairies, spirits, ghosts, and immortals were the "remains of a feudalist society" that didn't fit into the new revolutionary era. But to me, these magical "Once upon a Times" took me on an unfettered flight from which I didn't want to return.

Once upon a time . . .

I heard another voice joining me in this flight: the voice of my father. During the limited time he stayed at home, one of my father's favorite things to do was to tell us stories. Every afternoon, around seven or seven thirty, after we finished our supper, my father would pull from his bedroom—which was also his study—his dark brown rattan armchair and place it in the middle of the living room. My siblings and I would go grab our small wooden stools and put them in two rows around the armchair—my brother and I in front and my two older sisters behind—and wait for the story to begin.

Most of the furniture in our household was loaned to us by my father's work unit, Anhui Provincial Association of Arts and Literature, and thus all stamped with its red seals. But the armchair belonged to my father and didn't have such a seal. Whenever he was home, he would sit in the chair at his big writing desk either reading or writing. The original brown of the armchair had faded into a shadowy yellow, but its surface was smoother and shinier than when new. "It was the finest and strongest rattan," my father told us. "It would only grow more solid through wearing." In this old but sturdy armchair my father leaned back, his long legs crossed, his left arm resting casually on the armrest, and his right forefinger and middle finger holding a burning cigarette. Our eyes followed its light blue twirl of smoke as it curled up in the air before drifting out of the windows. When he stubbed out the cigarette and slowly put it down in a dark blue marble ashtray on the coffee table nearby, that was his signal. He would clear his throat, take a deep sip from his big brown ceramic tea mug, glance around at each of his four little children sitting with their chins propped on their hands, and ask, "Now, are you ready?"

We always were, eagerly yet patiently waiting for him to draw up the magical curtain. Once he started telling, he wouldn't allow anyone to distract or interrupt him. Everyone had to be very quiet, as he put it, to be in the *milieu* of the story itself. Whenever he saw fit to stop, without warning, he concluded the way a traditional storyteller always did: "Well, everyone, we stop right here. If you want to know what happens next, wait until next time."

With that, he slowly rose from his armchair, his eyes sweeping over each of us with an intriguing smile. Then he strolled back into his study and disappeared into his own world of stories. Long after he left and after all my siblings had gone to play, I would still be sitting on my stool, immersed in those characters and what had happened and wondering what would happen to them next time we met. Most of the stories my father told us, I learned later on when I started reading on my own, were works by authors of Asia, Europe, and North America. Without knowing it, I had been acquainted with characters and stories created by such authors as Tagore, Dickens, Hardy, the Brontë sisters, Balzac, Molière, Maupassant, Flaubert, Zola, Chekhov, Tolstoy, Dostoyevsky, Melville, Hawthorne, Mark Twain, and Hemingway.

These and other books were shelved in the pine bookcase standing in the innermost corner of my parents' bedroom. About two meters high and one meter wide, the bookcase had double doors, the lower half of which were solid pine wood and the upper half clear glass, through which rows and rows of hard cover and paperback books could be seen. The bookcase was built by my grandfather as a wedding present to his beloved son-in-law. My mother often said that the most expensive property they had was all in that bookcase: the major portion of my father's salary and royalties, which amounted to a few thousand yuan a month, was spent on books. Like my father's old rattan armchair, the bookcase was free of the red seal. It was another piece of furniture my parents could claim as their own. It was their priceless treasure which, my father often said, would eventually be passed on to all of us.

By the time I learned to read, however, I would be warned to stay away from the bookcase and its treasure. In the summer of 1966, with his own first big-character poster, Chairman Mao lunched an unprecedented wide-scale political movement with the intention of purging the Party of any possible opponents and enemies, using middle school and college students as its driving force. The movement would later be known as the Great Proletarian Revolution. Mao became the Commander in Chief who conducted numerous reviews of the students, now organized as Red Guards. There were around two million at each review. Those students, who streamed into the capital from all over the country, assembled in the middle of the night, filed in at both sides of the Tiananmen Square for ten kilometers from east to west along Changan Avenue, waiting to be reviewed and to catch a glimpse of Chairman Mao the following day or the day after. Their Commander in Chief, accompanied by Deputy Commander in Chief Lin Biao holding his little red book of Mao's sayings, would drive in an open jeep past tens of thousands of students who waved the little red books, screaming themselves hoarse, wildly shouting "long live Chairman Mao." Then they all went home to "make revolution"—to smash up everything that was old; they ravaged homes, wrecked schools, destroyed temples, and attacked any enemies or potential enemies of the Party and its leader.

The revolutionary whirlwind, raging in every corner of the land, dazzled and terrified everyone. Big posters and slogans covered walls and filled the streets, written on the lampposts and even on the roadways. Pamphlets and leaflets fluttered in the air, as cars with big loudspeakers shuttled back and forth broadcasting Mao's sayings. Party leaders of various ranks were escorted by the rebelling masses onto open trucks and paraded in public. They all wore dunce caps with humiliating slogans on their heads and placards on their chests with their names in black characters with big red *X*s through them. They would be forced to kneel, and were beaten and kicked while their arms were twisted backward by students. Other Red Rebels wielded leather army belts to whip these men and women mostly in their forties or fifties. The brass belt buckle struck their backs and heads with heavy thuds. Some of them would fall down, their hands clutching their heads while blood oozed between their fingers.

"Next, it will be our turn," I heard my father whispering to my mother one night after we all went to bed. They and my grandma were talking in lowered voices in the next room, but I could hear them. The images of those Red Guards and the bleeding faces of those in the parading trucks reeled through my mind and kept me wide awake and deeply worried. Some big-character posters were already put on the wall outside our complex, citing my father as one of the biggest "ox ghosts and snake demons" who were accused of using their novels and movies to engage in anti-Party and antirevolutionary activities. I knew it was only a matter of time until he would be hauled out for the mass denunciation meetings and street parades.

Then I smelled something burning. I got up and my sisters too. We tiptoed to the bedroom door and saw letters, notebooks, and photos piled up in our white enamel washbasin burning. My parents were squatting around the basin and sorting out letters and documents, sometimes tearing up pages from thick notebooks and throwing them into the fire. After the scorched paper burned thoroughly, my grandma, who stood beside the door as if on guard, sprinkled water from a smaller basin onto the ashes before shoveling it into the dust pin. My mother was holding a black-and-white photo, in which she wore a short-sleeve floral-patterned qipao (evening gown) and sat on a chair, smiling at the camera. She gazed upon the picture for a while and slowly placed it on the top of the burning pile. With a dull crackle, its edges began to burn. The photo started curling and then flattened out. In an instant, the smile was swallowed by the fire and the floral gown turned into ash.

"What about those books?" My mother sighed. My father shot a glance at us, stood up, put both his arms around our shoulders and said, "Go to bed, children. Do not tell anyone what you saw tonight, hear me? Now go to bed."

The bookcase. And all those books. What were they going to do about them? I knew these books would cause trouble for us. Since the goal of the revolution was to cleanse people's souls of any alien elements in order to develop a pure revolutionary mind, it was necessary to destroy everything that was old and cultural, produced in the pre–Cultural Revolutionary era. Books, of course, were considered particularly dangerous and deserved the most thorough scrutiny and extermination. They were one of the major targets during those frequent home ravages—expected and unexpected, organized or randomly conducted by zealous revolutionary loyalists, including Red Guards.

The first thing in the morning, I hurried to my parents' bedroom to check on the bookcase. It was still there, but with a different look now. Inside its double glass doors my father put a large piece of thick, brown kraft paper and on its outside, he pasted a huge poster of Chairman Mao smiling above the Tiananmen Palace. He also locked the bookcase and gave the key to my grandma. Under no circumstances, my father warned, could any of us open the bookcase and take any book out of it.

In the following days and months, Red Guards and other rebel factions from local and provincial art school and opera troupes, who wore red armbands and faded green uniforms and caps, would break into our house, smashing up antique porcelain vases, tearing up any books they found, searching anything they considered old or suspicious. They confiscated my father's collections of traditional Chinese painted scrolls, a rare collection of handwritten history volumes bound together by fine silk strings, and his two manuscripts.

My father wasn't at home to witness these ravages. He was going through sessions of confession and self-criticism in a secluded camp outside the city and would later be sent to the labor farm to have his thoughts reformed and soul remodeled. But the bookcase survived, thanks to the poster of a smiling Chairman Mao in front and the brown kraft paper in the back. Its survival, the very fact that it was still standing there with all its treasure hidden inside, gave me enough courage to go against my father's warning not to be anywhere near it. Every day, after returning home from school, while my grandmother was busy preparing dinner, I found the bookcase key at one inner corner of the first drawer of our chest where my grandma hid all the other keys. Carrying a small stool, I sneaked into my parents' bedroom and closed the door quietly behind me. I placed the stool beside the bookcase, stepped on it, and began peeling off the Mao poster; after that, I slowly rolled the poster over and carefully placed it underneath the bed. I opened the doors one at a time so that they wouldn't make any noise, and then all those books, about ten shelves in all, greeted me with a smile that rippled over their dusty spines. I pulled the stool over and sat down or sometimes stood on it, drawing one after another book, straight from their rows, from the top shelf to bottom, leafing through pages and stopping whenever I felt like it. To my amazement, I recognized many familiar faces and voices, the ones I had met and listened to in my father's storytelling. I conversed with these characters and listened to their stories for hours and hours, only to be interrupted by my grandmother's gentle yet loud voice calling us to supper.

In haste I put whatever book I was reading back in its place, closed both doors, used the paste my grandma made out of a mixture of sticky rice and water to reattach the Mao Poster, picked up my stool, and hurried out of the bedroom into our living room where my grandma was setting dishes on our big square dinner table. Guiltily, I rushed to the green plastic chopstick case hanging on the kitchen wall, grabbing a whole bunch and quickly dividing them into five pairs. Then I turned to the dish cabinet to get the bowls, again, five. It had been a few months since we all could sit together with our parents for our meals. I didn't even remember when the last time was that I needed to set up seven pairs of chopsticks and seven bowls. But now I didn't feel as sad or empty as I used to, preoccupied with that wondrous land I couldn't wait to return to.

From that land the characters kept coming back to me, whispering into my ears, in Arabian, Japanese, French, German, Russian, and English. Each voice told his or her dreams, fulfilled or unfulfilled, sweet or bitter, heavenly or hellish. These various human dramas—tragic, comic, tragically comic or comically tragic—crowded into my brain and helped to push away the constant worries and chaotic surroundings, offering me a glimpse into the strength of humanity—how much humans could take and still survive with grace and dignity. I now started looking around with newly acquired hope and faith, knowing that some day, maybe not too far away, things would go back to normal. Father would return home, sit once again in his magical rattan armchair, and tell stories; mother would finish her seemingly endless assignments and come back to us, and we would be allowed to read what we loved reading and to do what we enjoyed doing.

These characters and their stories brought me so much wonder, excitement, hope, and joy that I found it difficult to hold them all to myself. I felt like a river overflowing with words and stories, and then, on one of those quiet late afternoons when I sat on the stool in front of that pine bookcase, I decided that some day I would let the river flow out of me. I wanted to let these stories be heard. I wanted to hear my own voice as well as theirs.

Like my grandmother and my father, I became a storyteller too.

It all started on a rainy evening in the late fall of 1972, at a military farm on the outskirts of the city. It was my first year of middle school. Every semester, we would go to the villages, factories, or military training camps to "learn from peasants, workers, and soldiers," as called upon by Chairman Mao, who believed "petty bourgeois intellectuals" like us should go through thought reform at an early age. To better serve this purpose of thought reform, our school opened a branch campus at a military farm about sixty miles away from the city. We would spend one third of our semester there, undergoing military training and working in the fields at the same time. The dorm for girls was a vacant military warehouse where there were two rows of big communal brick beds padded with dry straw. About twenty of us slept on these beds next to each other, with about fifty centimeters of space each. On this particular rainy day, we stayed indoors instead of weeding the sweet potato field. We studied the latest of Mao's directives and exchanged our thoughts with one another, as our teachers asked us to. We soon became bored. After the teacher left, we gathered in groups of three or five and started chatting. A small black speaker in the corner of the room was broadcasting a snatch from the opera *Red Lantern*. The daughter of the revolutionary martyr was singing in solemn high-pitched notes as she vowed to carry on her father's unfinished cause. It was one of the eight revolutionary operas we grew up listening to. Each of us could sing every song and speak every line verbatim.

The rain kept rattling on the glass windowpanes and the air inside seemed to stand still. Yinping, a girl who had just transferred from another school and who never cared much about what others thought of her, stretched her arms and yawned, "Oh, my, so boring. I wish someone would cut off that damn wire of the speaker." The other girls and I nervously exchanged looks. But no one said anything. I was then one of the two monitors of our class and felt obligated to say something. "Let's get some rest, then. Tomorrow we still have work to do," I suggested. "What?!" Yinping burst out laughing, "Go to sleep? Now? Not even seven yet!" Other girls started giggling. Yinping seemed to be encouraged and continued, "I wish we could do something, anything." Then, all of sudden, she fixed her stare squarely at me. "I know your father is a writer, right? You must have heard lots of stories from him, right?" Before I could even respond, she hopped across two or three beds and landed on mine, the tiny brown freckles on the bridge of her nose turning red with excitement. "Yes, yes, maybe you could tell us one or two?"

The room suddenly became quiet. Raindrops gently tapped on the window; their steady beat seemed to soften the ear-piercing voice of the opera singer. Several girls started moving toward our direction, and before I realized it, they had formed a circle around me. I thought of those moments when my siblings and I sat just like that around my grandma and my father, waiting for the story time to begin. How long had those "Once upon a Times" been gone? How long since those voices had vanished?

I felt my eyes a little wet and heard my voice slightly trembling. "OK," I broke the silence, "only one, only tonight."

But that turned out to be the first of many times when I told stories, whether we were in the branch campus, villages, factories, or other military training camps. When we were back at school, I continued my storytelling, despite the limited time and constricted space. Every morning, our regular classes were preceded by a fixed fifty-minute reading period called the *daily reading*, a session strictly reserved for reading and reciting Chairman Mao's little red book—especially one collection entitled "Three Old Pieces." Regardless of levels and grades, every class in the entire school was mandated to have such a session. It was the class that started our day. Each student had to hold his or her little red book in front while reading it aloud. If anyone was caught doing something else, such as idling around, dozing off, or worse, reading for other classes, he or she would be warned at the first offense and disciplined or even expelled at the subsequent ones.

After these required morning reading sessions, other subjects, such as math, Chinese, physics, and chemistry, started piling up on us one after another, until four in the afternoon. The precious ten minutes between each class was all we had. Like my father, I broke down each story, so the audience would always have to wait until the next session. As soon as we finished our mandatory exercise during the first recess, all the girls rushed back to our classroom, sitting in a circle around my desk, urging me to continue whatever story I was telling. I remember it took me several weeks to finish the story of *Les Misérables*. One time, just as I reached the moment when Jean Valjean and Javert were standing face to face with each other outside the wall of the convent, the bell rang, but nobody moved. Dozens of eyes focused on me, waiting for me to go on. I looked over the crowd and saw our math teacher—who was also our homeroom teacher—standing on the platform, his eyes rolling with suspicion in our direction from behind his thick bottle-bottom-like glasses.

I cut myself short and whispered, "Teacher Wang is here. Wait until next time." I then quickly sat down at my desk, grabbing my math textbook and pretending to read. But somehow I couldn't concentrate. The teacher's seemingly penetrating eyes made me uneasy and nervous.

One hot summer afternoon I went home to find my mother, who had returned three days before for her monthly home visit, sitting on one side of the dinner table with my grandma on the other. Both looked worn out and worried.

"Your home classroom teacher visited today," mother said. Her voice trembled deep down in her throat. My heart started sinking. To any student, a home classroom teacher's visit usually meant trouble, mostly serious. A model student, who excelled in both academic and political performance, I had never had a teacher's visit until now. I waited anxiously for my mother to continue.

"Your teacher said you told stories to your classmates. Some are not good ones. Others should not be told at all. It is just not appropriate or acceptable for students like you to be involved in that kind of activity."

My mother paused, exchanged a perplexed look with my grandma and sighed,

"You have always been such a good child, so understanding and all. What got into you this time? Haven't you forgotten the old saying 'Disaster always comes from one's mouth?'"

My heart dropped with a heavy thud. It all came back—the warning that had been passed down to us, the warning not to tell, the warning that we grew up on. When my grandma told us not to retell those old stories, when my father forbade us to be anywhere near that bookcase, they must have acted upon this warning in order to prevent any possible disaster from descending upon their grandchildren. How could I forget this ghost-like warning? How could I think that I could tell whatever stories I wanted to tell to others? I closed my eyes for a few minutes, feeling caved in by a darkness in which I could see no end ahead.

It was a moment before I spoke again to my mother and grandma. "Don't worry," I assured them. "I won't tell anyone stories any more. I have been so foolish. Sorry." Holding my hands in hers, my grandma said: "Don't blame yourself. It's my fault too. Just be careful from now, OK?" I nodded; my nose felt a little sore, but I bit my lips to hold back tears. There was nothing I could or should say now.

Before I had time to act on my own, however, I had a major push from the outside, a push so strong that it would silence me for years to come. Not long after my mother's warning—and my teacher's, of course—a large-scale political campaign was launched; its goal was to wage battle against the spiritual corruption from Western bourgeois ideology and any sentiments associated with it.

Unlike other political movements, this one specifically targeted schools—from elementary through middle and high school.

The reason for this campaign was that certain manuscripts written by anonymous authors—probably very young ones—were found circulating among the students. Since 1966, with the exception of Mao's selected works, almost all the old books had been out of print and few new ones were published. For those who wanted to write books and have them go public, the only avenue was through underground transmission. Similarly, those who wanted to find books, any books other than Mao's works and a handful of revolutionary memoirs and novels, had to engage in clandestine activities—borrowing or trading books with each other, swearing secrecy, wrapping the books with innocent and harmless covers (such as pictures of heroes and heroines from the eight revolutionary operas or natural scenery). In this sneaky manner, published or unpublished books were passed from one person to another.

The manuscripts that were being circulated on middle and high school campuses were considered especially harmful and dangerous because the majority of them were romance and love stories, such as *The Maiden's Heart* and *Shaking Hands Once More*. In the lexicon of that era, the word "love" could be understood and interpreted only as loyalty toward the Party and Chairman Mao. Any other connotation would be threatening and corruptive to revolutionary minds. As a result, the meaning of love in its human sense was nonexistent; it became a forbidden and shameful subject for men and women, young and old alike, because it would only disarm and eventually destroy their revolutionary willpower. In the new society, people loved and married for the sake of revolution, and that was how the new plays and films of the time portrayed it.

As an initiative, school authorities nationwide called on all those who had read or heard about these underground manuscripts to come forward, turning in any such books in their possession or providing information for tracking them down. Those who had the books but chose not to turn them in would be expelled from school;

those who had read them, and thereby had to a certain degree indirectly helped "spread poison," were to engage in serious self-criticism and write letters to the school authority promising that they would not under any circumstances repeat their mistakes.

The scale of this campaign soon accelerated into another mobilized political movement that intended to purge schools of any "unhealthy, pernicious, poisonous" elements—from the feudal remnants of the prerevolutionary China to the bourgeois influence from the Western world. The folktales about those beautiful and witty fairies and spirits I heard from my grandmother would fit the former category while the stories I learned from my father and later on my own would fit the latter. To avoid any potential danger that might fall upon my family, particularly my father, who I knew couldn't afford to have any further troubles, I did self-criticism profusely during the class meetings for telling these stories and took the blame for my own foolish action. In both oral and written forms, I promised, over and over again, that I would be true to my honor as a model student and that I would never do anything that was incongruent with the revolutionary cause.

From that time on, I restrained myself from telling stories to anyone in school and didn't even want to talk much. Now and then, when a few of my neighbors' kids came to my house to play, they would plead with me to tell them some stories. I reluctantly obliged. Since they didn't go to the same school with me, I didn't have to fear their reporting on me. But this sneaky way of telling often made me feel guilty as well as nervous, even if we were at my house and those kids were my neighbors. The fun was lost; the sense of wonder was lost and, along with it, my own voice.

Before long, I stopped telling stories altogether. After graduating from high school, I settled down in my father's home village where I worked with peasants in the fields from morning till night with little time or desire to tell stories or even to think about storytelling. But the world of words was not completely lost. It was brought back to me by the villagers—men and women, old and young—who seemed to have endless stories to tell and could find any place to tell them. The revolutionary storm in urban areas had made little direct impact here in the village where the peasants labored from dawn to dusk in the most primitive ways of farming—backs to the sky and faces to the earth.

As a way to survive, they created their own world that was alive with the sound of human voices. At the end of each long day of fieldwork, either planting and harvesting rice or picking cotton, I would join the villagers who, whenever weather permitted, always gathered in the open courtyard inside the village ancestor hall. We would stand, sit, or squat on the stone steps, holding our rice bowls, and get ready to tell and listen to stories. Most of the villagers were good storytellers who could tell stories about everything—from the Silver River and down to the Lu village, from folktales of ancient times to the legends of different dynasties—it seemed to me there was nothing they didn't know or couldn't tell. One of those storytellers, who was one of my great-uncles, a man with rough dark skin and deep wrinkles on his wide forehead, could remember and act out every episode in the classic novels *Three Kingdoms* and *The Outlaws of the Marsh*. Each time he finished a story, he would, like my father, repeat the phrase, "Well, everyone, if you want to know what happens next, wait for the next chapter." Listening to him, I remembered the voices of my grandmother, my father, and my own, the voices that had been lost one by one in the distant silence.

Three years later in the late fall of 1977, about a year after Mao's death, the new leader lifted the ban on college admission that had been imposed since the beginning of the Cultural Revolution. Overnight, every new and old high school graduate, tens of thousands of them, ranging from ages eighteen to forty, who had been denied opportunities to pursue higher education for the past ten years, were now for the first time eligible to take the national entrance exams that might give them a chance to go to college. This sudden turn of events put everyone on edge. It was as if we had been plodding hopelessly through a vast desert and now suddenly saw the only oasis ahead. That was where hope perched; that was where life started. The competition among the exhausted travelers was frighteningly fierce, since no one was certain how long that oasis would exist and when it would disappear. Ten years' bitter and desperate struggle merely to stay alive made it difficult for us to believe in anything at all.

After two rounds of national written tests, I became one of the lucky travelers who finally approached that land of hope, my eyes moistened by its greenness and my thirst quenched at the sight of its clear-flowing water. With tears welling up in my eyes, I cheered, but I couldn't hear my own voice. It was shrouded in too thick a cocoon to break free, at least not yet.

It was in early March when I arrived on the campus of a small liberal arts college located near the Yangtze River. The dorms were still under construction. The male students, who outnumbered the female ones, moved into the only finished dorm. All the girls, about twenty of us, from different departments, English, math, physics and chemistry, would spend our first few months in college in a deserted Buddhist temple that had been recently converted into a temporary residence. The first days flew by as we were busy cleaning our beds and unpacking our suitcases and canvas travel bags. Here and there, I saw a golden sunflower hair pin, a piece of blue and white ribbon, a purple floral patterned hair band, although not yet any jewels. It would take a while for us girls, who had harbored for years both desire and dread over these girlish accessories, to realize that it would be safe now for us to show our feminine side without fear of being accused of pursuing a petty bourgeois lifestyle. Out with these small and simple girls' items came a little nervous yet much relieved giggling and laughing.

Night fell early in March. The spring was here, but the wind was still howling as if in its last attempt to show off its powerful presence. Not wanting to go outside, all the girls went to bed and climbed into our quilts—cherry red, sky blue, lavender purple, and sunflower gold, with stripes and floral patterns—and waited in silence for bedtime.

Lying down on my upper bunk bed, I studied those triangular crimson wooden beams that supported the temple ceiling. On their surfaces were exquisitely carved entangled figures of dancing phoenixes and flying dragons, gazing upon me from the ceiling with their weathered and mysterious eyes. Once upon a time, they must have witnessed the glorious days of this temple, with its worshippers flowing in and the incense forever burning. What happened to this temple? Where were those monks and worshippers? There must be so many stories hidden behind the eyes of these dragons and phoenixes. But who would know if no one was able to tell them? Who would listen to silence if that was all they could hear?

Then, as if to answer my questions, a voice projected itself into the quiet night.

"It is too early to sleep. It is too cold and dark to go outside. Can anyone tell us a story?"

The clog was unplugged; the water started flowing. It couldn't stop. The words, suppressed in my chest all these years, now billowed like the ocean tide washing over the shoreline. Like someone who has been living in a desert for years and who now for the first time approached the ocean, I plunged into its surging waves and swam with my arms wide open. Out of the water, I ran along the shore, inhaling fresh and cool ocean air, picking up beautiful shining seashells and watching the tide carry the fine silvery sand far away to the ocean depths.

I started telling stories once again. The temple was listening, the night was listening, and I was listening. I heard my voice flying out of the temple, like a bird with newly grown wings. Having toured around the sky and seen everything behind and beneath it, the bird flew back and alighted on my shoulder and stayed. I realized that I had left behind a long-forgotten warning—you must not talk. Disaster comes from words.

Yet, I do remember not the warning but the need to tell. My grandmother once told me, one story you tell or listen to gives you one more life to live. In listening to her and my father's stories and in telling my own, I live multiple lives and speak in a multitude of voices.

The following are some of those voices, voices of the people who, once silenced in the land of the Dragon King, now choose to remember, to tell, and to live.

槐花 2

The Fragrance of Huai Flowers

April. The sun, floating over the orange and purple horizon, gently sprinkled golden-red sparkles over the clouds coasting in the scarlet ocean. Like beautiful heavenly fairies waving their silk stream-sleeves and twirling their canopy skirts, the clouds danced all the way to the distant skyline.

The air was saturated with a ravishing fragrance, the fragrance of Huai flowers. Tracing the source of this fragrance, you would find yourself in front of a gigantic three-hundred-year-old Huai tree standing on the north side of a one-story-high grass-covered hill. From its long thick branches hang strings and strings of tear-shaped cream petals and green leaves. As the April breeze whispered by, these strings of leaves and flowers would sing and swing like many wind chimes.

Singing and swinging along with these wind chimes were about a dozen small elf-like children who laughed and screamed while tumbling under the tree or sliding up and down the green hill. When exhausted, they would climb to the top of the tree and sit comfortably on its branches that were solid like wooden benches, their legs dangling and rustling through cream petals and green leaves like fish swimming in a clear-watered stream, their little fingers fluttering in and out of the branches like butterflies. They picked, gathered petals, and then shoveled them into their mouths, from which a rivulet of

23

fragrance trickled out, winding up and down through the boughs, and encircling the hill with an intoxicating sweetness.

When dusk quietly settled in, this sweetness merged with the flavor of steamed bread, rice porridge, red bean paste bread, and salted cabbage. Parents started calling their children home for supper. One by one, reluctantly, these little elves jumped from the tree down to the hill, rolling on the grass for one last time, hurriedly filling their mouths and their pockets with more flowers, leaving behind them a trail of sweetness that stayed long after they were gone.

Among these elf-like children was a little girl who would always be the last one to leave. When she finally got back to her house about fifty yards away, she would place a wooden stool right beside the living room window and sit herself down, gazing out of the screened window at the hill. She had piles of small twigs and strings of Huai flowers on her lap which she wove in criss-cross patterns to create green and creamy wreaths. Behind her, she could hear her grandmother's steel spatula scraping a wok briskly while stir-frying snap beans, her two older sisters chatting about their school day, and her younger brother's toy machine gun firing. But to her, all the voices seemed to have receded. It was the most sacred and quiet moment for her, a moment when she could hear the grass whispering, the leaves singing, and the wind chanting, a moment when she could watch fairy clouds dancing with the setting sun, all the way to the distant rosy sky.

I watched the spring of 1965 fly by, following the dance of beautiful cloud fairies, listening to the laughter echo from the green hill, inhaling the air permeated with the freshness of morning dew and the sweet fragrance of the Huai flowers. That short sweet spring I left behind almost forty years ago formed an instant of time in which my life became strangely interwoven with that of another, an invisible being who, along with the setting sun, the dancing clouds, and the Huai flowers, evoked in me a sense of wonder that has enabled me to see and live each day with renewed hope and clear vision.

Toward the end of autumn 1964, my family started preparing for a long journey that would take us to a remote mountain area located eight hundred miles away from Hefei, the capital city where we were born and grew up. For the next two years, my father told us, we would have the opportunity to see what rural children's lives were like in the Dabei Mountain region where, because of its unique geographical location, it had been a battlefield during both the first and second civil wars between the Communist and the National Parties. Every inch of its soil and every blade of its grass, according to many war memoirs, was soaked with the blood of thousands of civilians—peasants who lived and died, most of them untimely, during the wars. It was shortly after the three-year famine from 1960 to 1963, following the Big Leap Forward, which in its blind frenzy to catch up with the West, had led the nation into an unprecedented economic catastrophe. Millions perished from hunger or hunger-related diseases, especially in rural areas. In an effort to appease the angered and disappointed peasants, who made up one fifth of the nation's population at the time, the Party launched another political campaign, calling for urban intellectuals, especially the artists, writers and poets, to "go down the village and up the mountain" and "experience life and write for the workers, peasants, and soldiers."

My father, born into a peasant family, had always regarded himself as one, even though he left his home village at the age of seventeen and later became a self-educated writer. The majority of his works—novels, short stories, and movies—had rural settings; the protagonists were very often the peasants who, historically deprived and marginalized, bore the heaviest burdens and treaded the toughest road in silence and with endurance.

Partly in response to the Party's call and partly, I believe, in answer to his own genuine concern about the peasants and an artist's compassion to tell stories about their lives, my father volunteered to serve as the secretary in the Party Committee of Yinchao People's Commune in Yuexi County, the heart of Dabei Mountains, where he had visited many times before and where he had written one of his best-known movies, *The Wind and Snow in the Dabei Mountains*, a story about two families' ordeal during the second civil war between the Communist and the National Parties. In the late fifties and early sixties, before 1966, father would spend at least five to six months every year in those mountain villages, living and working with the local peasants who had inspired the best of his writings.

This time, however, was different. He was not alone. He brought along with him the whole family: my mother, my grand-mother and us four children. He even arranged to have our city residential permit changed to that of rural residence, which meant that if by any mishap we couldn't change it back, we would all become peasants permanently. As a result, we were to stay there for the rest of our lives, losing all the privileges city children would have. And back in the 1960s and '70s, even through the '80s, the difference between life in cities and in rural areas was that between paradise and hell. We were, however, too young to realize what kind of risk my father was taking upon himself and us. As far as I was concerned, paradise and hell seemed to blissfully become one in the spring of 1965, in a sweet, scary, and yet heavenly way.

The journey was a long and treacherous one. Our vehicle, a minivan assigned by the Party Committee of my father's work unit to transport us to the Yuexi County, was packed with three adults, four children, two big suitcases, and two travel bags which were stuffed with our winter coats. My mother and grandmother spent night after night sewing these coats, filling the inside with new cotton to brace us for the harsh winter in the deep mountains.

In an early dawn in the late fall of 1964, our van rumbled out of the city onto a jagged mountain road, leaving our city home farther and farther behind. After initial excitement, we all became quiet as our van wobbled and jolted along. On one side of the vehicle were the overhanging rocks chopped flat as if by a sharp blade of a knife, and on the other was a cliff overlooking the steep bottomless valley. Through the rattling windows, we could see pine forest surging up and down alongside of our vehicle which rocked back and forth like a tiny boat adrift in a vast wavy green ocean. The driver, whom we called Uncle Yu and who had been telling jokes since we hit on the road, was now intensely quiet. His back was bent over his wheel;

both his hands grasped the wheel tightly; his knuckles were strained and turned to a dry white. It was as if a single wrong movement would cause the car to lose its balance and roll over the edge.

We felt nervous too. My father tried his best to help us relax by telling us stories, mostly about the places he had once lived and the people he had befriended who were struggling to survive. He sat with his back leaning against the tightly closed window and his face toward us. Now and then he pointed at some distant top of the mountains and told us that those used to be some of the major battlefields where now were buried thousands of local peasants and their families, who had been killed by both White (Nationalists) and Red army (Communists) soldiers. He reminded us of how lucky we were to live in the city, having many privileges rural children would not have. They didn't have brick houses to live in like we did; they didn't have rice to eat; all year round their major sources of food were sweet potatoes and corn. The majority of them, my father pointed out, didn't even have schools to go to.

We listened while dozing off. My father's voice was like some kind of familiar yet strange music hovering over our ears; although we couldn't quite get its outline or sketch its metrical form, we did feel the heaviness and seriousness in its tone.

After about twelve hours' travel, shortly after dusk, we finally arrived at Shiguan, a small town where the office of the County Party Committee was located. We slept through most of our journey and were carried by our parents, still sound asleep, into our new home and awakened the next morning to a strange yet refreshingly pleasant mixture of melody: birds twittering and warbling, water murmuring, and leaves rustling in a gentle mountain wind.

Our new home, provided by the county government, was one of ten adjoining bungalow apartments which, inhabited mainly by the members of the County Party Committee, sat at the foot of a mountain. They were all identical units, with red brick walls and gray-titled roofs, their doors facing the south. Each unit had a small yard about ten meters away from its front door, a yard that was fenced in by bamboo branches on all sides. The yard in front of our unit, which was at the east end of the row, was unfenced, except on its south side, where it was bordered by a grassy hill. At its foot was a narrow mud road that ran in parallel with a small river across which bigger wavy hills could be seen crouching like big animals whose gaze fell gently upon the small hill on this side.

The hill, higher than our apartment, shaped like a cone with a flat top, reminded me of tombs I had once seen when visiting my father's home village, although with one major difference. On the top of those tombs was placed a clay bowl into which families regularly put food to pay their homage to the dead. Instead of the tribute bowl, the top of this hill was shaded by a gigantic tree, its long and leafy boughs reaching out all around the hill, holding it in its arms, like a mother who was slightly bending forward while helping her child get ready for the first step.

That was a Huai tree, grandmother told us. When spring came in early or mid-April, it would be full of creamy white flowers with such a strong fragrance that you could smell it ten miles away. She used to live in a village before moving to the city at the age of ten. There were three or four Huai trees near the entrance of her home village, my grandma recalled, none of them half as big as this one, yet when they bloomed the whole village was steeped in a sweetness that lasted for days and days until the end of April. These flowers, she told us, grew on tiny thin twigs, each about three inches long, on which tear-shaped leaves and petals were strung evenly on both sides with one single leaf on the top. She and other girls called these twigs "wishing twigs." Whenever they wanted to make a wish or even make a bet, they would pick one and count its leaves and petals one by one, starting from the bottom. When you reached to the top, if the number you counted happened to be an even number, then you won that wish.

"Like a fortune teller?" my oldest sister, Shuni, asked.

"Well," my grandmother was trying to find an appropriate word to answer the question when my father chimed in.

"Oh, yes," he grinned, "Do you know how to write the word Huai? It is a combination of a tree and a ghost. You'd better be careful what you wish for, girls." My father said, laughing, "The ghost is hiding in the tree and he knows everything." "Ghosts?!" We burst out in excitement and started firing one question after another toward my father: "What do they look like?" "Why do they hide in the trees?" "Will they come down from trees?" "Will they hurt us?" My father chuckled, raising both his arms up in a gesture of surrendering, "OK, OK. One at a time. Now, first question, what do they look like? Let me think." My father sat down on a chair behind him, his arms crossing over his chest and his eyes looking up at the ceiling as if he were waiting for some answers to fall from there. My grandmother patted him on his head and turned to us. "Don't listen to your Baba. He is kidding you. No talking about ghosts. You will have nightmares."

She then continued with her fond memory of those sweet-scented Huai trees. What was more, she went on, their cream petals were also delicious to eat. In early spring, the time when the stored food was consumed and newly planted crops had yet to be gathered, the villagers would mix the flowers with wheat or sweet potatoes flour to make pies as their meals. "We would climb up the Huai trees and stuff our stomachs and then our cloth bags with petals so that our mothers could make pies or porridge." As she recalled those sweet moments, my grandma clucked her tongue as if she were already chewing those sweet petals. "But it is now only October. You need to be patient," grandma said. "Wait for April." We nodded, already feeling a sweet liquid burst onto our tongue and melt inside us.

With this sweetened expectation, we started our new life in Yuexi county as rural children. After my father went to Yingqiao People's Commune to assume his duties as a Party secretary and mother began her work in the county Committee office, we were left mostly to ourselves. While my two sisters were at school, my brother and I helped our grandmother with gardening: pulling weeds, loosening the soil, planting and watering tomato, cucumber, and hot pepper seeds. Most of the time, we followed our neighbors' kids, running wild down the dusty country road, along the bank of the river, through the woods and bushes on the large and small hills nearby. Our favorite place was, of course, "our little mountain," the hill that nestled in the arms of the Huai tree. The older kids loved climbing branches and straddling them while waving willow sticks as if they were gallant knights riding horses. We younger ones, who weren't tall enough for those branches, were content with staying on the hill, climbing up and rolling down, over and over again.

Once a boy, about five or six years old, who had cherubic cheeks and big dark eyes, decided that he too could ride one of the horses like bigger kids did. He managed to climb onto one of the lower branches but lost his balance and fell heavily on the grass. He sat there with both of his legs spread out crying. He wiped tears away with the back of his soiled hands and smeared his face with black dirt and gray sand dust that made him look like an opera clown. We couldn't help laughing, though we felt sorry for him. He cried and cried, cursing and complaining until the older kids told him that on that Saturday, they would take him to the bigger mountains to pick berries and to see rabbits or even foxes. The promise immediately brightened his stormy face. His big round eyes opened wide and his two little tiger teeth jumped out as he smiled from ear to ear.

Like this little boy, we would all be delighted to go to the bigger mountains. When my father returned home from Yinchao every two weeks, he always took us to go hiking in the ranges of these neighboring mountains where we could listen to the wind whistle through pine trees; smell the fresh bamboo shoots and walnuts; pick red, purple, and orange wild berries; chase small animals like rabbits, squirrels, and sometimes, even foxes; and scream at the top of our lungs to hear our echoes reach far away to the next mountain top.

But to father, the trip to the bigger mountains meant much more than an outdoor fun activity. Each time he took us there, he would bring us to one of the highest peaks of the main range, where, on a newly cleared space, stood a tall granite memorial tower on which was engraved the inscription: "Long Live the People's Heroes." It was surrounded by several rows of marble tombs with names on them, the tombs for the high-ranking Red Army officers who died in the wars—the anti-Japanese war (1937–45), and three revolutionary civil wars in the late 1920s, early 1930s, and late 1940s. Further away from these tombs were scattered, far and wide, numerous small shabby piles of brownish dirt, with a rough shape of triangle. They remotely resembled the tombs in my father's home village, but were much smaller and more dilapidated. There were no bowls of tribute, no names, no tombstones. Whenever we passed by these small conical mounds, my father would pause and ask us to do the same, explaining to us that in these unmarked tombs were buried the local people who were killed by both White and Red army soldiers. Nobody would ever remember them, but we must know and remember, he said. "Many children can only live underground forever."

His low and somber voice, punctuated by the wind roaring above the sea of pine trees, sent a chill down my spine, which made me miss terribly our little mountain where we could race up and down as wildly as we wished without fearing that we might disturb someone resting in his or her tomb. What was more, of course, we were closer to the Huai tree and our dreams of a sweet spring.

As time went by, the sun set earlier and days grew shorter. The birds' chirping became thinner and the leaves' rustling dwindled into a quiet whisper. Once the sun sank down behind the darkening horizon, the air seemed to be shivering in a frosty silence. Through the window, I watched dry, yellow leaves whirling in the air, floating cautiously as if looking for a good place to settle down. Still in a tender, although lighter, green, the hill opened its arms to these drifting guests and embraced them with its warm greenness, the greenness that promised yet another spring.

Shortly after supper, we went to bed and huddled in our cotton rolls, watching the fire in the stove simmering in the dark, listening to the wind wail and to the hungry wolves and bears howl from the distance.

We listened and waited in the midst of coldness for spring's return. Every day, when we passed by the green hill and the bare boughs of the Huai tree, we would stop and look for any signs. When we saw red-breasted robins and black-tailed magpies tentatively flying down to the grass looking for food, when we heard the ice on the river cracking up with the flowing water, and when we touched tiny green buds dancing timidly in a warmer and gentler wind, we knew that spring was almost here. "See these buds?" Grandmother asked. "Before you know it, they will spread all over the tree." Many nights after I went to bed, coiling up in my cold cotton roll, I imagined those tear-shaped creamy petals fluttering in the air and its fragrance wafted into my sleep and sweetened my dreams.

Then one day, at midnight in early April, these sweetened dreams were interrupted, suddenly and chillingly, by the unexpected intrusion of a distant being. I use the word "being," because I cannot find any other word to describe this strange yet familiar presence. I heard a voice, a heartbreakingly tender voice, like that of a very young child, letting out a deep groan as if releasing his pain and fear into the dark night. Then the voice stopped, as suddenly as it started, although its echoes still hovered over the dark silent sky.

I sat up, both my eyes and ears wide open. Everybody was sound asleep, deepening the quietness of the night. Holding back my urge to scream, I stared nervously through the window into the darkness outside, which blocked all my vision and prevented me from looking farther than the shadow of the cone-shaped tomb-like hill, which was staring at me through the dark in silence.

The first thing next morning, I asked my bother and sisters if they heard such a voice. No one took my question seriously. My oldest sister, who was in the fourth grade at the time, explained that there might be some smaller animals who, unlike wolves or bears, were still starving and crying for food after a long cold winter. When I ventured to say that it didn't sound like an animal and that it was more like a young child's voice, they all laughed it away.

I didn't laugh, feeling confused. I even pinched my arms to make sure that I was not hallucinating. Yet, if the voice were real, why didn't my sisters and anyone else hear it? Or, maybe, maybe, that voice was just reaching out to me only? If so, whose voice was that? A real person or some kind of ghost?

Before long, these questions gave away to a much anticipated excitement. My grandmother was right; within a few days after that first bud, strings and strings of creamy petals were frolicking all over the tree. Every afternoon, as soon as my sisters returned from school, we would rush up the hill to the Huai tree. Like care-free birds we flapped in and out the green leaves, now hiding behind, now popping out, grimacing and giggling. The older kids climbed up the tree; after locating a strong branch to sit on, they started picking flowers and throwing them down to us younger ones, who sat on the grassy hill, trying to catch as many sweet-scented petals as possible and stuff them into our mouths as fast as we could. Sometimes, I would bring a big bamboo basket, fill it with flowers and take it back to my grandmother. She would make delicious pancakes with a mixture of the flowers, sugar, sesame oil, and flour.

After filling our stomach with the sweet flowers, we used the hill slope as a slide, climbing up and rolling down, over and over again. When we got tired, we would lie down on the grass, hands behind our heads, watching the sun swim over the golden waves of clouds, counting and naming each cloud as they floated across the sky—a dragon, a tiger, an elephant, a cat, or a bird. I always imag-ined these clouds to be beautiful fairies who would fly down from heaven any time to our earthly paradise and share our fun of flower picking and eating. We would hold on to this paradise as long as we could, until the dusk brought our parents' shouting from the dis-tance: "Come home! Supper time!" The calls would usually go sev-eral rounds before they could take us away from the hill and the tree. Finally, we sensed the growing impatience in our parents' voices and hurried down the hill, waving to one another, promising that we would be back soon, for another day of sweetness.

It was during one such sweet moment when I once again heard that familiar voice and felt the presence of that being.

It was another beautiful sunset. A few clouds were wandering across the blue and rosy sky. The golden twilight shone upon the clear waters in the river and over the wavy hills on the other side. A little tired from all that rolling and tumbling, I lay down on the grass near the tree to have a little rest, watching the clouds slowly move closer to me and feeling the gentle touch of the grass on my face. It was then I heard that tender voice again. It seemed to have risen from within the hill, spiraling its way up to the tree, lingering in the air for a while before it flew away like an invisible bird into the distance. I sat up, my heart pounding. Some of my companions were on the tree and others were sitting on the hill. Nobody seemed to hear anything. I kept quiet and continued listening, with a certain expectation I couldn't explain. But the voice seemed to have flown away and didn't return.

That evening, my father came back from Yingchao. He hadn't been home for almost three weeks now. He looked very tired, his thick black hair a little ruffled and beard unshaved. His eyes had deep dark circles from lack of sleep. He sank heavily into his rattan armchair and let out a deep sigh. My grandmother, who was busy preparing supper, mildly scolded her son-in-law for not taking good care of himself.

"Look at you." She pointed at my father's shirt. "You are bone to bone, now, so skinny. No good."

"Ma, don't worry. I am fine. At least I won't die of hunger. Those folks are still dying there, you know. There was little I could do to help them." He stopped himself abruptly when he saw me approaching. He reached out his big hands to me and in an instant, I was lifted up and found myself sitting right on his lap, laughing while dodging his scratchy beard tickling my neck and cheeks.

"How is my baby girl doing, if I may ask?" Father teased me, his face now loosened up with a big grin.

"Can I ask you something, Baba?"

"I'm all ears, my dear." My father patted me on my head; his eyes glinted with a gentle smile.

"Remember what you told us about the word Huai, it is a tree and a ghost?"

"Yeah, I guess. And?"

"Is there any real ghost at all? What do they look like?"

My father looked at me, a little surprised: "So, it was you who asked that first question." He thought for a few minutes and continued. "Well, I don't really know. I've heard many stories about ghosts. Some of the ghosts are real. Others not. They are all different. Just like us. Good and bad, young and old, I suppose."

"What is a good ghost?"

"What is a good ghost?" my father repeated my question and paused a while before he spoke again.

"Well, good ghosts, we can say, are just like those we call nice people, good-natured and kind-hearted. Their lives were often cut short because of the wrongdoings of others. They are the saddest ghosts because they know they are forced to leave the world not in their due time, so they dream of returning again."

He stopped and sank into silence, his eyes shifting toward the window and gazing beyond. His mind seemed to have already wandered away, maybe to one of his books he was writing. Working as a Party secretary in Yingchao had taken much of his time and energy, but I knew he was also trying to finish a novel at the same time. He was about to say something more when my grandmother interrupted us with a basket of hot steamed buns. She put the basket in the middle of the table and said,

"Don't talk about ghosts to the kids. They will have bad dreams."

My father grimaced at me as if saying, "I will tell you more next time."

The next day was Sunday, a clear bright spring day. My father had been sitting at his desk since morning, writing. It was one of those rare Sundays when he could be at home working on his book. After lunch, my two sisters went to a neighbor's house and my brother was about to take his nap. Telling my mother that I wanted to go up the hill and read there, I took one of my favorite picture books and headed out.

I slowly climbed up the hill and sat down under the tree; with my back comfortably leaning against its solid trunk, I opened my book and started reading, or rather, looking at the pictures. It was very quiet around the hill. Younger children were napping and the older ones had their own gatherings. The only sound was the leaves gently rustling in the breeze and the pages flipping. Now and then, I picked a string of huai flowers hanging overhead and chewed the petals.

Then, all of sudden, I heard "Boo!" and a yellowish light flashed before my eyes for about a second. Then I saw that on the opened page of my picture book was sprinkled all over fine grains of sand, glittering like gold in the sunshine. I thought someone was playing a trick on me and that he or she must be hidden somewhere behind the tree. I yelled, "Who did this? I saw you! Come out! I saw you!" I looked around but couldn't see anybody. Everything was as quiet as before. I thought it might be someone passing by who threw sand over my book, but whoever did this, he or she was down the hill and I was up. How had the sand so precisely and evenly scattered on my book? Also, that person had only one place to hide—on the back of the hill. But the sand seemed to come from my front, where there was an open road and not a soul to be seen.

I tried to continue reading my book, but when I turned over another page, "Boo!" There it went again. The fine shining grains of sand spread evenly on the page, covering only the picture part so that I could still read the words. I touched the sand and then, slowly, I tipped the book and in an instant, the sand streamed into the grass and disappeared, like a small creek merging with a river and never to be seen again.

Then I heard that voice. That painfully sweet voice, now half-crying half-laughing. It was hard to tell which. Again like last time, it seemed to have come from deep down the earth, the inside of the hill. Its echoes hovered over the hill and around the tree before it disappeared into the green leaves and creamy Huai flowers.

And as suddenly as it came, it was gone. I strained my ears to listen to that voice one more time. But it would not come—at least for now. By this time, my little mind believed that someone wanted to tell me something I didn't know. It was this innocent and persistent belief that made me decide I would wait. He must be somewhere, up the tree and around the hill. Even if I couldn't see him, he was there and could see me. And I waited.

And I waited. Afternoon turned into dusk, dusk into night.

I waited. April turned into May and May into June.

Days became longer and hotter; the Huai flowers started falling off, covering the top of hill with creamy tear-shaped petals, and quietly emitting their delicate fragrance into the now hot and humid air.

But he didn't return.

The first week of June, my father received an order to leave Yuexi county. There might be some major political movement in the city, and he was told to go back immediately. Within two days, we had everything packed back into the same vehicle that brought us here a little less than a year before. On the day of our departure, around sunset, we closed our door and went to our yard, saying good-bye to the now colorful garden with the green cucumbers, red tomatoes, green and white gourds, yellow hot peppers, and the thriving golden sunflowers my grandma had planted. For the last time, my sisters, brother, and I climbed up the hill. We sat down under the Huai tree, breathing in the fragrance of the petals scattered over the grass and chatting about all the fun time we had spent on the hill and under the tree.

Then my father came. He was holding a big bouquet of wild flowers and placed it gently right beside the tree as if he were afraid of awakening someone.

"What are the flowers for, Baba?" We were all curious.

My father squatted beside the tree, adjusting the bouquet into an upward position.

"For all of them."

"Who?"

My father stood up, his face shadowed in the darkening glow of the setting sun.

"You should know this, children." He cleared his throat and continued.

"This hill is a tomb. A whole family was buried right here underneath your feet, children, altogether nine people. The oldest was eighty years old and the youngest was only six at the time. They were all executed by the White army during one of the raids because two of the men from the family were Red Army officers."

"Why didn't you tell us before?" Shuni, my oldest sister, asked.

"Actually, I just learned it myself. The County Party Committee were planning to expand this road. They were going to demolish this hill. It was then they found out."

"What are they going to do with the hill, the tomb, then?" I asked, feeling suddenly chilled and panicky for someone I vaguely knew as if only in dreams.

"I don't know, children, I don't know. There is nothing we can do. We must hurry. Once it is dark, the road will be too dangerous."

Without saying another word, he turned around and slowly walked down the hill, followed by four of us, one by one, all holding our breath, afraid of disturbing those who we now knew were resting underneath us.

I was the last one to leave. And when I finally did, I knew I didn't go alone. I was taking with me that presence, that voice, that being. I left the hill with him. I made two small wreathes with the green twigs and cream-colored petals, like many I had made while sitting beside the window watching the sun set and cloud fairies dance. One for him and the other for me. I placed one on the top of the green hill under the tree and held the other close to my heart. Then I picked up a string of cream Huai flowers and tiptoed down the hill.

The same van took us back through the wavy green sea of pine trees toward home. From then on, we, everyone in the family, would be thrown into a stormy ocean in which we would struggle for more than ten years before we finally reached the shore.

Throughout those years living in constant fear and pain, I often had dreams in which *he* came to me. A young boy who looked like the one who cried when falling off the Huai tree branch, with the same rosy cherubic cheeks and big round eyes. Only he wasn't crying; his mouth seemed open, but no sound came out. His head was crowned with a wreath of green leaves and cream petals of Huai flowers; his deep and clear eyes looking into mine. I walked toward him, my hands reaching out. At first he was startled, but then he smiled. I saw his lips trembling and heard him whispering in a sad yet sweet tone. I have listened and still listen to that voice, telling me stories that I can never fully understand but will always appreciate.

The spring of 1965 flew by and through me like a river of sweet fragrance. Every April, when Huai trees are in full bloom, bursting into the air with that dreamy fragrance, I know he is standing there on the top of the hill, under the Huai tree, watching me. I think I know what he is trying to say to me.

I think I know.

槐花 3

Pear Flower Alley

For those of us who grew up between 1966 and 1976, everyday lives were plagued with unspoken and unspeakable uncertainty and fear. As the windstorm—the Great Proletarian Cultural Revolution—ravaged the land, political chaos became personal reality. In order to survive, people went through endless confession and remorse, retracting their sayings and reporting to the Party about their own "misdeeds" and those of others. Like ants in a hot frying pan, they frantically rushed back and forth to big and small meetings, advocating rebellions and trying to prove their loyalty to the Party and its Great Leader.

As long as one was considered to be in line with the Party, and thus in that of the Leader, one would have a chance to survive. The struggles that allowed for only a few survivors turned everyone into enemies. People were constantly pushing into and stamping on each other, killing and being killed, cursing and being cursed, violating and being violated. But brutality and violence were merely secondary to a patterned existence. Our faculties lost their natural functions. We had eyes, but couldn't see; we had ears, but couldn't hear. Our eyes could focus only on one direction and our voices could utter only identical syllables in unison. It was a mapped-out existence to which we were destined and from which we could see no hope of escaping.

But every now and then, hope did come. For me, it came in the form of a small alley. Like a river it flowed away from the caged life, taking me on a ride to a space where hope could bloom and dreams grow.

Caught in the whirlpool of the fierce political storm, we, as children, could hardly hold on to any such space. Our residence complex, once our childhood paradise, now turned into a hellish and brutal public battleground where physical torture, home ravaging and mass denouncement meetings became a daily routine. The bamboo forest garden near the entrance, where we used to play hide-and-seek, was now flattened by large bulldozers. In its place, Chairman Mao's statue now stood, as everywhere else. Every time we passed by the statue, we slowed our steps and kept our voices down. With his eyes looking up and right arm pointing toward the sky, the great helmsman seemed to have cast an invisible net over us, a net from which nobody could break free.

Least of all could our parents break free. Now categorically condemned as "reactionary bourgeois intellectuals," they became one of the central targets of the Cultural Revolution. Every day, at sunrise and sunset, my father and other residents, most of whom were writers, film-makers, actors, poets, musicians, and painters, would line up in double rows. Each holding the little red book with his/her left arm, bowing at ninety-degree angles toward Chairman Mao's statue, they began their ritual of qing zui, pleading for forgiveness for their alleged crime against the Party and the state. Members of the revolutionary committee—army personnel and members of the Worker Propaganda Team—stood by to ensure that the ritual was conducted sincerely and faithfully.

Every morning on my way to school, I had to pass by that file bending at the waist in collective obedience toward the statue. I never looked up at any of them, nor did I want to be within earshot, knowing well that I would only be haunted later by those blank and ashen faces and those monotonous and hollow voices. Like someone who was being chased by a sweeping flood or crushed by a mudslide,

I fled through the entrance without daring to look back as if a single glance would freeze my legs and cage me where I was.

The street outside the entrance was no better, merely another cage, packed with bicycles, wheelbarrows, flatbed carts, occasionally cars and trucks, and pedestrians fighting fiercely with one another to get through. My companions and I, the weakest people among all these competitors, hand in hand, holding our breath, were bumped back and forth by the wooden handles of wheelbarrows and the metal handlebars of fast-running bicycles and swept to and fro by the silent and sullen-faced adults who brushed us aside with cold stares and shoulders. During those few minutes of trying to get across the street, we were at the mercy of a threatening and fierce adult world with only our own survival instinct to protect us.

But once we crossed the street and turned into a narrow winding alley, we knew that the tormenting journey from our complex through the entrance into the street was coming to an end. The alley, a short cut on our way to school, had a beautiful name, Pear Flower Alley. It was a three-meter wide path paved with shining flagstones. Though without a single pear tree or any other fruit trees, it was to me an orchard where the most colorful fruit trees grew and the most beautiful fruit flowers bloomed. The fruit trees were the various stalls lining both sides of the alley and the flowers were the residents standing behind the stalls, waving and smiling to us as we passed by. Their voices, loud and joyful, echoed throughout the alley: "Morning! Kids, watch your way! See you back here! " We waved to them in return; the very word "back" gave us enough courage to face another chaotic and fearful place at the other end of the alley—our school.

Each day in school was a dread and a torture. Ever since 1966, schools, like everything else, had been turned into chaos and confusion. College and middle school students were mobilized by Chairman Mao and the Party as a shock force during the earlier stage of the revolution. Called upon by Chairman Mao to destroy the old world, embodied in the Four Olds—old ideology, old culture, old habits, old customs—they abandoned classes and were organized into Red Guards or other rebel groups. They donned red armbands and took to the streets, raiding homes, looking for any remnants of a traditional society such as books, art, ceramics, or anything Western, writing big-character posters condemning the guilty and holding struggle sessions, denunciation meetings, or street parades, one after another.

As the escalating violence turned universities and middle schools into arenas of chaos, elementary schools, though still open, were no longer fit for study. Teachers either had been denounced or were organizing their own rebel groups. Classes were frequently disrupted by students who acted rebellious, shooting paper bullets from their slingshots at the teachers, cursing the teachers who ventured to give any assignment. These children, who usually came from red backgrounds such as the ruling class of Party members, workers, and cadres had nothing to fear. Teachers, concerned with their own political security and worried about their own safety, didn't bother or dare to interfere. For me and several others from our complex—known as He Da Yuan, The Black Courtyard, because most of its residents were "reactionary intellectuals"—the vicious verbal attacks were common and seemingly accidental pushes or shoves frequent. I knew better than to fight back. No matter what happened, I followed the teachers' example: to keep my mouth shut and to be on a high alert all day in order to avoid an attack or, if attacked, a confrontation. From morning until late afternoon when school finished, I never let down my guard so that I wouldn't get hurt and humiliated.

My tightened nerves would relax only when I approached the Pear Flower Alley on my way back home, when my heart would light up and get ready to fly, knowing that I was now stepping into a magic place where I no longer had to lower my head and fold my wings. Along with my companions, we flew by each fruit tree, taking in the delicate fragrance of each bloom, and picking up flowers of various colors as we went along. We glided over its smooth flagstone surface, laughing while chasing each other in the bright sunlight.

About sixty meters long and three meters wide, the alley was flanked with twenty or so stalls which were set up right in front of the owners' front doors. Most of them were craftsmen who could make a variety of handicrafts. Among them were the man who braided purses of various colors and sizes with plastic ribbons, the man who knitted yarn with lucky charms such as red paper lanterns and small toy zongzi (pyramid-shaped silk pendants), the man who wove square and round cricket and bird cages with thin bamboo strips, the man who could magically transform flour dough and sugar paste into figurines, puppets, and dolls painted with various opera masks, and the man who blew musical notes from reed whistles and bamboo flutes.

And then there was the food. From golden toasted peanuts, to black watermelon and silver sunflower seeds, from white cotton candy to amber-colored sugar paste, from red ice-coated cherries to green dried bamboo leave–wrapped dumplings. We would visit each one of those residents, watching them as they worked on their crafts, tasting their food, listening to and chatting with them, laughing about stories and jokes they told us. By the time we reached the end of the alley, my pocket money, usually several cents my grandma gave to me, was all gone. In its place was a heart unloaded of its burden, ready to fly again. In the midst of a turbulent stormy ocean, the Pear Flower Alley became a peaceful island where we found our way back to a once lost childhood and were given chances to see the world through a kaleidoscope of colors instead of just blue and black.

Sometimes we wondered how strange it was that the Pear Flower Alley was spared the horrendous revolutionary torrent. Neither Red Guards nor any other revolutionary rebellious cells had set foot in the alley, destroying the old to build the new as they had been doing everywhere else. While all the streets in the city were shedding their names because they were not revolutionary enough— Willow Road, Confucian Street, Heaven's Dragon Road, and Lotus Lane were now called Anti-Revision Road, Anti-imperialism Street, The East is Red Road, and Loyalty Lane—the Pear Flower Alley was still unusually called by its old name despite the fact that it had been officially renamed Red Star Alley. The reason for its survival, we heard from people both inside and outside the alley, was that the alley was believed to be haunted by ghosts who had been protecting its residents from any outside harm. Not fully comprehending the meaning of those rumors about ghosts, we treasured this paradise where we too felt secure and protected.

During those pleasant moments of interacting with those residents, we were showered with the warmest and brightest smiles rarely seen in the outside world where the adults' faces were either frosted with cold or frozen with fear. We became friends with almost all the residents, who knew our names and who our parents were. They even referred to us as "kids from the Black Courtyard." They said in such a loving and amusing tone that it magically swept away a sense of shame that had been hanging over our heads like a dark cloud ever since the storm started. The sugar flour man asked me many times to pass his regards to my father whose movies, he said, were among the best he had watched. He never forgot to add, "Tell him, you must tell him, think far ahead. Just remember, there is always a road that can take you out of a mountain. A cart can always find its way to turn the corner. Heaven would never close all doors. Do you understand what I mean?" Yes, I do. I had witnessed on a daily basis, directly or indirectly, various attempts by those intellectuals who wanted to end the pain once for all by ending their own lives. Some succeeded and others failed. But every day the attempts were made and lives were lost. As children, we could only stand aside watching those tormented souls soaring like curls of smoke into air, hopelessly anticipating that there might be a time when our own houses would be burning.

If the sugar flour man reminded me that there was still hope for us to escape from that fire, my other friend taught me how to laugh away my fears and anxieties. She was in her early sixties, of a small build, with a loud and clear voice and a never-fading smile on her wrinkled face. Her stand sold toasted peanuts and sunflower and watermelon seeds, which were the finest and crispiest in the whole alley. She mixed fine golden grains of sand with peanuts and seeds in a black wok on a brick stove and slowly stirred them with a big steel spatula until peanuts turned into golden brown, the seeds silver and black. Then she used a bamboo colander to filter out the sand, separated the peanuts and seeds, and piled them up in two round bamboo trays. We could smell their fragrance everywhere in the alley. It was her secret, she said, grinning at us like a little girl, that she could toast nuts and melon seeds just perfectly—neither burnt nor underdone.

She sold these nuts and seeds in paper cups she folded herself, in the shapes of small boats, lanterns, shoes, or rabbits with big bellies. For all the filled cups, regardless of their shapes and sizes, she only charged three cents. But what attracted us more to her stand was the whole procedure of nut- and seed-toasting and paper-folding. Her hands, sinewy and chafed, were slightly shaking, but her fingers could always hold firmly whatever she was working on. A plain piece of paper came alive in her hands and flew into ours filled with tasty seeds. We would either swiftly eat up the contents or pour them into our pockets and beg her to make another boat, lantern, rabbit, or even a doll. She would just smile, picking up another piece of paper and asking us what we wanted this time. The fact that we often ran out of our cents to pay never bothered her. "Pay me back whenever you remember," she told us, "Don't worry about it. You kids shouldn't worry too much. Just have fun here."

We had great fun with her, learning from her how to fold animals and other objects, chatting with her and listening to stories about her or about anyone she had known in her past. From what she told us, we knew that she was alone and that she had a son who was married with a young boy, and who was still working as a farmer in the countryside. "When I've saved enough money," she said, "I will bring my grandson here to the city so that he can go to school like you."

Like most residents in the Pear Flower Alley, she had moved to the city from the countryside many years ago and settled in the alley

as a town dweller who earned her living by selling handcrafted articles and food. One of the stories she loved to tell about the alley had
something to do with its name. The story went that long, long ago,
many poor but beautiful young girls and women had lived there.
Officials and warlords in the city, who had money and power to do
whatever they liked, paid frequent visits to the girls and women.
These visits often occurred after the curtain of night fell which hid
behind it whatever it intended to hide. When the morning sun drew
up the heavy dark curtain, it revealed only a deeper and heavier
silence that wouldn't go away with the night. So time went by, until
one morning, when one of these girls was found dead in a pool of
blood—she was shot in the head, people said, by a warlord who was
furious at her refusal to serve him. The girl's name was Lihua—Pear
Flower. It was not her real name; it was given to her by an elderly
woman who brought her from a southern small town to the city.

Not long after Lihua's death, the alley became haunted. People
swore that sometimes they saw one, other times several, shadows all
dressed in white, dancing on the surface of the shining stone path.
As they twirled around, white pear flower petals fluttered around
their swirling sleeves and flashed through the dark air.

We didn't give much thought to the gossip about ghosts, nor
were we afraid. These ghosts, who were believed to appear only in
the pitch dark night before sunrise, seemed to us far away, somewhere beyond our reach. We did, however, feel the presence of one
ghost-like figure in the alley. Whenever we passed by a small and
low-roofed house around the corner near the other end of the alley,
we would slow down, trying not to make any noise. Walled by a
mixture of sun-dried mud bricks and brown dry rice straw, the house
looked like a cave. Its entrance, a faded red wooden door, always
remained ajar, revealing a hunched figure—an elderly woman—sitting motionlessly in a small light-brown bamboo chair. Her pale face
flickered in the heavy shadow of the darkness.

Nobody really knew anything about this woman. People had
different stories about her mysterious life. One story went that she
was a landlord's wife—probably because of her pale complexion, an

indication of people who could afford to stay indoors without having to work in the field—and that she had escaped to the city after the land reform started and her husband was executed. In another story she was married to a National Party army officer when very young, but her husband didn't have the time to bring her with him to Taiwan when the Communists took power in 1949. Whichever story people believed, one thing was certain: she lived by herself, never talked with any other residents, and was never seen stepping outside of her door into daylight.

Though sometimes wondering about this mysterious shadow, we managed to keep our distance, for fear of disturbing whatever spirits might be hidden in the silent darkness. Meanwhile, as each day in the outside world became increasingly chaotic, we seized every minute and opportunity to stay longer and longer in our own safe space where we could forget what lay ahead of and behind us.

Then in early March 1970, word spread that the Pear Flower Alley was to be demolished for some construction site. All the residents would have to move. A loudspeaker was mounted on an electric pole at the entrance of the alley, blaring every day with the order to move out of the alley so that construction workers could flatten their houses. We were fearful for our friends who we knew would have nowhere to go except returning to their home towns, most of which were located in remote rural areas.

Yet, despite the uncertainty generated by the threatening and fierce voice from the loudspeaker and the interference of the Revolutionary Committee which had become the only administrative office in effect since 1968, no residents were seen preparing or packing. It seemed that they were waiting for some miracle to help them stay. They were fearful, but also oddly hopeful. Every day they still put up their stands, arranging their crafts and food in the same way, smiling and waving to us as we passed by.

"Don't worry about us, kids," my friend with the toasted nuts and sunflower seeds told us one day, after she finished folding a little boat and filled it to the brim with black watermelon and silver sunflower seeds and handed it to me.

"A boat can float anywhere. As long as there is water. We will be fine." A faint smile glinted on her weathered face and disappeared into her short gray hair.

"But where would you go if the alley were gone?"

"I don't know, kid. There must be somewhere we can go."

"But where? You can't go back to the countryside, right?"

She finished folding another paper; this time, it was a crane. Holding its long and graceful neck in her left hand, she used her right forefinger and thumb to draw open its wings back and forth. Then she gave the paper crane to me and again smiled. "Don't worry yourself so much, child. As I said, grass can grow and birds can fly everywhere, you know?"

I tried but couldn't smile back to her. My heart felt heavy with worry and uncertainty.

Each of the following days passed by with a tension lingering in the air. The construction teams, along with their trucks and bulldozers, appeared not far from the entrance of the alley. Several men with wicker safety hats and red armbands strolled back and forth outside the alley. The residents watched their movements vigilantly as they guarded their doors and stands.

Then a strange thing happened. Around the end of June, the deadline for the residents in the Pear Flower alley to move out of the alley, a huge storm poured from the sky and raged for three straight days and nights. On the morning of the fourth day, the sun came out, shining upon those flagstones with a dazzling blaze. The word went around that ghosts, about five or six of them, were seen dancing in the rain on the third night of the storm. On the fourth morning, when the storm had stopped, people said they saw pear-flower petals scatter all over the stone path, glistening with raindrops in the morning sunlight and billowing like a misty body of water.

Whether people believed it or not, from then on, nobody talked about the construction plan any more. Nobody moved. And nobody dared to challenge the residents to move, not even the District Revolutionary Committee. When I started middle school, I had to go by a different route, but I visited the alley as often I could. As I grew bigger and taller, the alley seemed to become smaller and narrower, but no less alive and joyful. The sugar flour man's dough figurines and puppets were wearing new masks and costumes; the bamboo man's cages were now filled with real crickets, and sometimes even birds; the flute-player now had someone who accompanied him with an erhu, the Chinese violin; and of course, our friend's toasted nuts and seeds were as crispy and tasty as ever, while her paper-folding became even more creative and colorful. Even that old woman sitting in the dark, for the first time, stood up beside her small bamboo chair, her body leaning against the frame of the shaky wooden door, her pale face emerging from behind the darkness, smiling curiously toward the morning sunlight and toward us.

It must be the work of those ghosts, I supposed. Whether they were real or not, it didn't matter. Those ghosts or spirits, lingering over the threshold of life and death, had tried to bring some kind of message. It was up to us to listen to and interpret these messages. They were there to protect and help people who were helpless as they themselves used to be. How ironic that we, who saw the sun rise every morning and were allowed to live through the daylight, needed help from those who were presumably from a dark and unclear underworld. Thanks to those ghosts, the Pear Flower Alley could flow freely through a muddy land. Riding on its silver water and flying over its sunlit waves, I, at least for the moment, broke free from that caged existence we were all condemned to live. And along the way, I learned that there is indeed such a thing called hope.

Jade Rabbit

Chang-O, or the Moon Lady, used to be an immortal who lived with her husband, Houyi, in the Palace of Heaven. Because Houyi shot down nine suns, sons of the Emperor of Heaven, he and Chang-O were driven out of the Heaven to live on earth. Eager to return to the Palace of Heaven, Chang-O drank in one gulp the medicine for immortality her husband received from the West Celestial Queen Mother as a reward for his bravery. But when her body began flying up toward the sky, Chang-O lost control and landed at the Moon Palace instead. It was a cold and lonely place. The only company Chang-O had on the moon was a little white rabbit named Jade Rabbit who was guarding an osthemus tree. Every day and night, whenever Chang-O became homesick, missing her husband and her friends on the earth, Jade Rabbit would dance for her around the osthemus tree, offering her a glass of wine he made from its flowers. As time went by, Chang-O grew attached to Jade Rabbit. Every August 15th, in the middle of autumn, they would sing and dance together around the moon. We would watch them from earth and know why the moon was so clear, bright, and full on that day.

To me, the time when the moon became clear, bright, and full was also the time I could be with my own Jade Rabbit, the one and only cat I had ever kept, taken care of, loved, and then eventually lost. In his quiet and gentle way, Jade brought to me the warmth and tenderness much needed for those cold and dreadful days.

Jade came to us at a most uncertain time, the summer of 1967. Every corner of the country was burning with revolutionary flames; people became maddeningly restless, blindly rushing to and fro, not knowing what to fight for or against, but still constantly on the run for fear of being left behind and swept away by the revolutionary torrent. As the fighting among various rebellious cells became more intense and fierce each day, the city was turned into a battlefield; streets and buildings were sometimes used by different armed revolutionary groups as blockades from which they would fire at each other.

To ensure that we kids were away from dangers, my parents decided to send us to my grandparents who lived in Bengbu, an industrial city in the northern part of our province, about four hundred miles north of Hefei, the provincial capital where the fighting was the worst. Not long after we arrived at my grandma's, she took me and my brother to visit one of her closest friends whose cat had just had five kittens and who asked if we wanted any. Glancing casually at the cozy straw-padded bed where the mother lay, a golden striped cat, and her five tiny babies, I saw him—a snow white fluffy ball—all white except a pair of light gray eyebrows and a light gray tail. I had never seen a white cat before—all the cats I knew were black, golden, gray, or a mixture of these colors. I stopped right beside him, observing him more closely. Now standing up, a bit shaky, on his four tender paws, he was also looking at me. Before I knew it, I heard myself pleading to my grandma, "Can I have this white kitten?" My grandma was a little surprised, but her friend seemed to be amused.

"Good choice, my dear little Sanzi [Number three]. He is a lovely baby."

Reaching her hands toward the kitten, she scooped him up and placed him in my palm. He timidly lifted up his eyelids and mewed in a soft voice as I held him with my arms. In that instant, I knew—maybe he knew too—that we had both found a friend.

The day after we got home with the new member of our family, my grandfather built a small square wooden house and my grandmother sewed a light blue cotton-padded roll with patterns of tiny stars. The kitten circled back and forth in his new house, his gray eyebrows rising with curiosity and his tail swaying with contentment. Every now and then, he would look up at us, mewing once or twice as if expressing his thanks. "Such a good kitten," my grandma patted him fondly, "like a little Jade Rabbit." At this he mewed again, as if in response to the words my grandma had just uttered. "Yi, you must have liked the name. Jade Rabbit?" my grandma asked. To our amazement, he seemed to nod and mewed again.

From then on, we called him Jade Rabbit, or simply, Jade. Wherever he went and whatever he did, Jade carried with him a certain calm and comforting glow that often reminded me of a full moon in the clear autumn sky. Unlike many other cats, he didn't take to fish, which made him free of the fishy odor most cats had. His favorite food was also ours—steamed buns—one of the most delicious snacks my grandmother ever made. My brother and I often ate together with Jade. We would chew one piece of the bread after the other and then handed it to him. He would watch us very patiently as if he knew we would never betray him by swallowing his food.

By the end of the summer, we had to leave for home since school would restart soon. My grandma said that Jade was too young to travel and that she would send him over to us as soon as she could. With that promise, my brother and I packed to take the train home with our grandfather. My grandma and Jade came to the railway station to see us off. The noon sun was cascading down onto the cement floor of the station overcrowded with people rushing back and forth, all looking panicked and anxious as if in a constant fear of missing their trains. They were running, screaming, and bumping into each other without bothering to look back. The trains, as always, were packed with people pushing into one another, stepping on one another's feet, tearing off one another's buttons, shouting insults and curses. The burning heat, it seemed, scorched the last ounce of patience out of this crowd and turned it into a restless and agitated mob.

But Jade seemed not in the least to be disturbed by the surging crowd and the madness it generated. He squatted in the hook of my grandma's arms and watched those frenzied people rush by, his big brown eyes gleaming like mirror-still water. His calm was contagious—we didn't run with the others, twisting our arms through the thick crowd and trying to get on board, like we used to do. Instead, we stood there, waiting for the wave of the crowd to recede. When the locomotive's steam whistle blew for the third time, Jade mewed as if signaling to us that now it was time for us to go. As my grandfather pushed my brother and me on board, I turned around and waved to Jade, whose small white body rose over the black-haired crowd like a full autumn moon floating above a dark cloud.

Jade didn't come to us as soon as my grandma would have hoped. While my grandma was busy running back and forth between her home and ours, Jade stayed with my grandfather to keep him company. In June 1969, two weeks after my grandfather died a sudden and mysterious death, my grandma returned to us, bringing Jade along with her. He was two years old now, very strong and masculine-looking, with his white fur clean and shining more than ever. His eyebrows had become darker and thicker, and his eyes, smiling as before, seemed to be shadowed by a heavy sadness. He recognized us right away and responded to our calling him by squinting his eyes and waggling his tail. But he clung to my grandma all the time, following her wherever she went; most of the time he was just watching her, helping her with various errands. My grandma didn't have to tell him anything. He was all too familiar with her unuttered command, offering his service in a precise and timely fashion: to hold his own tin can for my grandma to fill with food, to pick up the iron hooked bar and pass it to her when she was clearing the stove ashes, or to hand her a palm fan to drive away mosquitoes. We were amazed by this incredible bond between them, to the point where we started wondering if Jade would ever want to know or get close to us as he had our grandma.

But Jade soon proved our worries unnecessary. Before long, Jade Rabbit found his way into our life. He became our big helper in keeping us warm in the chilly winter, at a time when we didn't even know that there was such a thing as a heating system. In the bedroom my grandma and we shared, there were two double wooden beds and one single bed—my grandma and I slept on one and my two older sisters the other. The single bed was for my little brother. Padded with a thin layer of cotton sheets and covered with equally thin quilts, all the beds felt like an icy patch in the winter nights. It always took a lung-shaking scream and a teeth-chattering shiver for us to get ready to dive into our beds. And once we did brave ourselves into it, our legs would immediately coil up near our chests, and remained in the same position all night long so that we wouldn't have to be near the rest of the freezing cotton rolls.

Every night, before our bedtime, my grandma would boil two kettles of water—no more than two, since the coal was rationed and had to be used sparingly—and pour the hot water into one oval-shaped bronze bed-warmer. After she twisted the lid tight so that water would not splash out and burn us, she placed the warmer inside each of our quilts—four of them—in turn. After one quilt was warmed up, the warmer went to another and yet another. By the time we went to bed, the warmer had lost much of its heat source and so had our quilts. The whole night, we had to curl our legs and arms together to preserve as much heat as we could in order to sleep through the bone-breaking chill.

Before long, Jade became, voluntarily and lovingly, a substitute for the bed warmer. He would sleep with each of us for a while, until we were warmed up, and then went to another roll, and came back again. His clean and soft body gently snuggled in our arms; within a few minutes, the warmth from his body spread all over inside the comforters. He would lie there until my sisters, or my brother, started calling, "Come here, Jade, come here. It is my turn now!" Jade would look apologetically at whomever he was going to leave behind, with an I-will-be-back-soon expression, before taking off for another heating mission. Because of Jade and his ever-present warmth, to sleep in our icy beds was no longer a dreadful torture; we looked forward to it every night with excitement and delight, as if there were fairies for us to visit and a sweet dreamland to go to.

Though quite masculine looking, Jade was by nature very shy and quiet. He was the only cat I ever ventured to or even was eager to play with, before him and after. No matter how often we teased him, or provoked him by tickling his neck or his paws, he would never lose his temper, like many other cats would do. Nor would he show any impatience when playing with us. My brother was often fond of caressing his white fur in the wrong direction, making him look like a small curly-furred lion. Yet Jade would stay put until my brother's attention turned to something else; then he would lick his hair slowly and stretch himself with relief.

As if he knew how dull those days were, Jade graciously provided himself as a source of entertainment. Once a week, my grandmother gave him a bath, which was one of the moments of fun for us. Before the bath began, my grandma filled the big round wooden bath tub with lukewarm water while Jade waited quietly beside the tub. We all squatted around, with basin, towel, and soap in hands, waiting for the order from my grandmother who was holding one of Jade' front paws so that he could keep his balance in the water. As the first water came pouring over his body, my grandmother would always say something like, "Look at you! Where did you get all this dirt, huh?" like she would to a little naughty boy who had got soiled from playing outside. Jade would lower his head, trying not to look my grandmother in the eyes. With his white fur soaked and dripping with soapy water, Jade was now more like an ugly monkey. Watching him get a bath often gave us a long and good laugh; he never seemed offended, as if he knew it was a rare fun moment and wouldn't take it away from us.

When my grandmother went back to her own home for a short period of time, we would take turns feeding Jade, which was not a difficult thing to do. We usually cooked some leftover rice with small dried and salty fish and put it into his tin can, since we didn't know how to make steamed buns like my grandma did. What was difficult, however, was my mother. After my grandfather died and my father was sent to a labor reform farm, my mother seemed to have a nervous breakdown, especially when my grandma wasn't with her. Sometimes while she watched us feeding Jade, mother would suddenly burst into tears and storm out of the room. She never touched Jade and always kept a distance from him as if he were some kind of ghost. Once my brother and I were chasing Jade around in the house, all the way into my parents' bedroom. Mother was sitting on her bed, silently weeping; our old family photo album, the one with a green floral silk cover, was lying open beside her. It was on the page of her family picture: my grandfather, grandmother, two uncles and mother, all smiling at us from a distance.

My brother and I, not wanting to disturb our mother, tried to leave the room. But Jade didn't move. He was staring at the family picture, his eyes watery. My mother stopped crying. She glanced at Jade, and then turned to us, her voice trembling: "Can you take Jade away? Let him go, please. I don't want to see him. I can't. Do you understand?"

Jade remained still for a while before he quietly retreated toward the door. We followed him, upset, but not surprised. Jade was with my grandfather during the time of his death. Mother had been shunning Jade ever since he came. Later that day, at the dinner table, everybody was eating silently; there was only the sound of chewing and our chopsticks clicking. Mother, all of sudden, broke the silence and asked, "Where is Jade? Did you send him away?" Without getting any response from us, my mother started searching the room with her eyes. "Where is Jade? Didn't I tell you to send him away?"

Where was Jade? We started looking for him, but couldn't find him anywhere. Mother charged into our bedroom and started ruffling the bed sheets, one after the other, and bending over to check. Suddenly, she stopped in front of the big bed shared by my grandma and me, her body freezing in an arc. We all went close and stooped over to look. Then we saw Jade. He was standing in a far back corner of the bed, looking pleadingly at my mother, his body shivering in the dark shadow underneath the bed. My mother's back remained frozen in the same bent posture for at least five minutes before she stood up and slowly sat down at the edge of the bed, without saying a word.

Uncertain what my mother would do next, we quietly left the room and hurried over to clean the table, my sisters stacking dishes and bowls and carrying them to the public tap forty meters away to wash them, I cleaning the table and sweeping the cement floor. When we finished our chores and went back to our bedroom, mother was still sitting at the bed, only now with Jade nestled right beside her. Every now and then he lifted his head and mewed in a whisper to my mother, who bent over to him, listening.

My grandmother, after settling all the business at her home, came to live with us permanently. She never fully recovered from my grandfather's unexpected death and was sometimes like a sleep-walker who had yet to awaken from a horrifying nightmare. She often sat on the edge of our wooden bed with Jade sitting either on her lap or right beside her, two silent shadows in the dark. Long before we woke up and after we went to bed, when all the lights were off, I knew they had been and would be sitting there, keeping each other company, speaking to each other in a silent and dense language we couldn't comprehend.

Not long after my grandma's return, Jade started showing some signs of a change in temperament. At first he was just brood-ing, refusing to eat anything that was not made by my grand-mother. Then he more frequently stayed out, restless and careless. He would go out for whole nights and come back with his white fur stained with dirt and mud. For the first few weeks, my grandma gave him baths, as before, scolding him for being a bad boy. He wouldn't look up at any of us; he kept his eyes downcast and his body shrank to almost half of his original size in the soapy water. We could no longer laugh as we used to. Our hearts were filled with bewilderment and concerns for Jade. But as with our grandma, we didn't know what to do. As each day went by, Jade seemed to be losing control, letting himself slide down a hill with no intent to return. Instead of his usual calm and cheerful nature, he became gloomy and moody and often looked confused and hurt. His eyes lost their sparkles of wonder and his tail became too heavy to waggle. His pure white fur now turned grayish and almost brown. He was getting thinner and thinner; my grandmother cursed over and over again but to no effect. Then she didn't say anything more. Whenever Jade sneaked back into the house at dawn and lay wearily beside the table or the stove, my grandmother would pick him up and put him on her lap, gently caressing his fur. The two of them would sit together until we finished our breakfast and went to school.

We all worried about Jade, wondering what had gotten into him that changed him so drastically. Through it all, my grandmother kept feeding him, washing him, but less and less would she talk to him as she had used to. It seemed that both were exhausted and both understood the source of this exhaustion. While Jade was busy running wild and my grandmother was busy trying to reform him, we were busy growing up and preoccupied with our teenaged interests and concerns.

Finally, when Jade attempted to catch the chicks raised by one of our neighbors, my grandmother couldn't tolerate his behavior any more. The decision was made and Jade was to be sent away to one of my mother's friends whose parents lived in the countryside and needed a cat to catch mice.

So off Jade went. He was about eight years old. On a quiet and hot summer afternoon, similar to the one when we first met him, Jade was gone. When we returned from school, the house felt eerily empty. My grandmother was cleaning the tin can she had used to cook for Jade since he was three weeks old. Then afterward, she wandered aimlessly in the kitchen as if not knowing what to do with it. I tried to take it from her hand, but she wouldn't let it go. Together we sat down beside the dinner table, staring at the empty can as if it were some magical box out of which Jade would pop at any minute.

In the heart-pounding silence my siblings and I started eating our supper. Our feet were hopelessly dangling over the crosspiece under the dinner table, reaching out to the empty space Jade used to occupy. The steamed buns were still warm, but we didn't need to chew and give them to Jade anymore. After supper, we helped clean the table and opened our books on it and began doing homework; we left the center uncluttered—that was where Jade used to sit, watching all of us, his soft brown eyes smiling and his tail waggling.

Through the glass window I could see a silvery moon emerging from behind a cloud on the dark blue charcoal canvas of the sky. I looked up toward the moon, and whispered, "Jade Rabbit." I then heard a soft "Meow . . ." and saw Jade scurrying over the silver surface of the moon toward me. As he approached, I held out my arms, grasped one of his front paws and shook it as I would a human hand.

槐花 *5*

The Voices of the Winds

Feng: 风 a noun, meaning "wind." In its philosophical sense, it is often associated with chi, an interior strength essential to the well being of the human mind.

Feng: 疯 an adjective, describing a mental derangement. As a noun, feng is caged on the top and left side by the radical for "sickness." Trapped within the cage of sickness, the wind, or chi of the human body, is deprived of a crucial outlet—the top where the head is and the left where the heart is—for it to blow at its will. As a result, it twirls and swirls inside, causing a loss of balance which inevitably leads to a breaking down of one's internal order and turns that person into a fengzi, a crazed being.

According to my grandmother, fengzi could be divided into two major types: wen fengzi and wu fengzi. Wen fengzi were those who turn their craziness inward; they are usually withdrawn from the outside world, licking their wounds alone, guarding with intense caution and fear whatever secrets they might have hidden. These fengzi, my grandma said, were the gentler kind. Just leave them alone. They won't harm anyone. A wu fengzi, on the other hand, is wild and dangerous. Never come close to a wu fengzi, my grandmother warned us. "You will become a monster if you are near one." Both fengzi, wen and wu, she said, are like different types of wind. Some are breezes, some are storms, and others tornados. "They have

63

to let this wind loose in some way," my grandmother sighed, "or it
will destroy them."

It was one of those gray, gloomy summer afternoons. The sky in
those days seemed to remain the same color: a sort of livid gray, covered with a tapestry of thick clouds, like a gigantic cataract stretching
languidly across the vacant eyes of the sky. In a voice as gloomy and
heavy as the overcast day, my grandmother warned us seriously on
that afternoon to stay away from those fengzi, both wen and wu
fengzi. "There are more and more of them, do you know? They are
everywhere. You'd better watch out." My grandmother's warning
didn't go unheeded; I did watch out, or rather go out and watch
whenever opportunities came up. I tried to trace the path upon which
each different wind or fengzi traveled, listening to their voices, picking up fragments left behind by those demented men and women
and wondering, often in vain, from whence these fengzi came and
where they would be going, if ever they would be traveling forward.

The wind, that is.

One of these fragments I gathered came from someone who fit the
category of wu fengzi. He was in his mid-twenties, but had already
lost much of his hair, with what he had left fringing over his ears like
a woman's hair band. He was always dressed in a faded grass-green
army uniform, an outfit that became popular after Chairman Mao
wore it when he reviewed thousands and thousands of Red Guards
on the Tiananmen Palace. On the left side of this wu fengzi's
chest—where the heart was—were pinned four or five of Mao buttons, metal, plastic, and even porcelain ones which lined up like
armor shields. With his left arm bent at ninety degrees, he tightly
pressed Mao's little red book to his heart while his right arm rose up
and down every five minutes, and he shouted with a shrieking voice,
"Long live Chairman Mao! Long live Chairman Mao!"

He took the street as the central stage where he was the one
and only actor. During the rush hour when we came back from
school and adults returned from work, he was always right there in
the middle of the major downtown intersection, dashing through the

crowd, bumping into bikes and tricycles, sometimes blocking one or two vehicles, shouting and singing. Whenever he sang lyrics like "Dear Chairman Mao, you are the red sun in our hearts" or "East is red, the sun is rising, there is born in China a Mao Zedong," he would add a shrill operatic chant, imitating drums, gongs, and cymbals: "Dong Chang-Dong Chang-Dong Dong Chang . . . !" Chanting to these words, he would start dancing the Loyal Dance, a dance performed by millions and millions every day everywhere as a routine demonstration of their loyalty to the Great Leader. He capered and sidled about, waved his hands above his head, kicked his heels, swung his legs, and bent his waist, all the while stretching his arms forward and then withdrawing them back to his heart, suggesting that his heart was always open to the sun and the sun was always shining in his heart.

Not many people knew who this man was, and no one really cared. He was just one of the many crazed people at that time. But I knew that he had been one of my friends' teachers of fine art and music at the 7th middle school. While painting the portrait of Chairman Mao for a giant poster, he accidentally spit some black ink on the red sun that was shining over Mao's head. Horrified, he tried desperately to erase the stain, but before he could undo the damage, one of his students saw it and immediately reported to the school authority. The teacher was arrested and thrown into jail on the charge of trying to ruin the image of the red sun—Chairman Mao—and was sentenced to three years. When he was finally out of jail, neither the school nor his wife wanted him back, a very common situation during that uncommon time. Everyone was desperately trying to show their loyalty in order to survive; the last thing they needed was to associate with an anti-Mao and an antirevolutionary.

Shortly after he was released from jail, people said that he attempted suicide by slashing his wrist with a razor, but the moment he saw the blood, he became hysterical, screaming while jumping all over his apartment stained with his own blood. Another teacher living next door saw the blood streaming through the crevice beneath the door toward the corridor and called the ambulance. The man was then rushed to the hospital and by sheer luck, according to the doctor, "picked up a life."

But this life was no longer his. He became restless and rootless. After leaving the hospital, he never returned to his unit. The street became his new home where he lived and performed. Policemen tried several times to force him back to his residence and to other shelters, but as soon as he was led to any roofed and walled space, he immediately started howling and wailing, scratching and slapping his face and neck until blood started dripping. Then on seeing his blood, he would become even more disoriented, bumping his body against walls. Fed up with his hysterical and violent self-torture, the city policemen decided to let him go running wild on the streets.

Once he was let free into the open air, his whole body became an angry whirlwind as if driven by an invisible airflow that had a will of its own. He seemed unable to stand still, even for a second, always running, jumping, hopping, dancing, or singing. He usually looked unaware and ignored the large crowd following him. But sometimes, he could become irritated when the crowd was too close to him or when children shot paper bullets with slingshots or threw small rocks at him. On a few occasions he turned around unexpectedly and charged like a cornered ox toward the crowd. The frightened children fled like startled birds.

Several times, the show became dangerous. Once, a little boy imitated him by making a strange sound and then pointed his figure at him, laughing. In a split second, the man picked up a pebble from the sidewalk and threw it at the boy who started screaming while hopping away, a thread of blood trickling down his forehead. Glaring at the boy with bulging and burning eyes, the man let loose a hair-raising howl that swept through the crowd like a gust of fierce wind.

My grandma was right. A wu fengzi like this one is fearfully dangerous. Yet, while it was horrifying to hear the voice of such a wild wind, it was even more so to hear that of a dead silent one which, like a wandering ghost lost in a graveyard at midnight, would freeze one's blood with a bone-breaking chill that never completely went away.

In the fourth grade, we were asked to form after-school study groups that met two or three times a week at one of the classmates' homes so that we could help each other with homework. My group was at the home of Rong, one of my closest friends at school. As we sat round a square dinner table in the living room studying, her mother, a well-respected obstetrician in the Hefei City Women's Hospital, always came to us exactly at the right time, either asking us if we wanted any snack or if we needed some help with the homework. It seemed she could read our minds—whenever we started feeling a little tired or hungry, she would appear from kitchen holding a large glass tray on which cookies, crackers, and candies were piled up on small glass plates. Watching her sea-green floral skirt sway as she walked, breathing in the fragrant scent of her honey and almond facial cream, listening to the lilt of her soft southern accent, and showered by her sweet smile and cheerful greetings, we felt like little princesses waited upon by a beautiful fairy godmother.

When we returned from the summer break for the new semester, Rong told us that her mother was not feeling well and that we needed to move our study group to somewhere else. But Rong told me that she hoped I could still come and study at her home. She said she was afraid to be alone and that her mother scared her.

"What do you mean?" I asked. "Your Mom? Scared you?"

She turned her eyes away and murmured something incoherent. I didn't see her tears, but I felt my eyes moisten; I didn't hear what she said, but my ears burned as if with scorching flame.

Through her tearful mumbling, I gathered what had happened to her mother. In a routine assessment and investigation conducted for her mother's application for the Party membership, it was found out that she had not been "honest" and was therefore "disloyal" because she didn't put the names of any of her overseas relatives on the forms as she was supposed to. As a punishment, she was immediately removed from her position and assigned to clean the sickrooms, hallway, and restrooms. She cleaned as well as she delivered babies, but sadly, each time she finished cleaning, she would either stand in the middle of the hallway staring at the passersby or lean against the door of the sickroom or lock herself in the restrooms. About a month ago, the hospital authority dismissed her from hospital on account of her "incapability to serve people."

As I listened, my heart sank. Although I didn't have any overseas relatives, I did know many who suffered because of this "black tie" to the "overseas imperialists." For those who chose not to tell and were found out by the authorities, the punishment was severe. Some were arrested and thrown in jail for an indefinite time; others lost their jobs in the city and were sent back to their homes of origin, mostly in rural areas. The thought of Rong's mother at least staying in the city and being close to her home was more or less a relief. I reached out to my friend and held her hands, trying to cheer her up. But Rong was still crying quietly and softly; her tears kept trickling down her face, her eyes averting mine.

What Rong didn't tell me then and what I found out later was that her mother had turned into a fongzi. If the art teacher had released all his fury and craziness into open air, Rong's mother chose instead to shut herself away from the outside world. After she was dismissed from the hospital, she refused to leave her house, not a single step. And she didn't talk, either. Not to anyone, not even to Rong's father. She was losing her memory, her energy, and her mind. Rong and her father watched hopelessly as she slipped away from them to a distant land of silence.

On Rong's pleading, every day after school I went to her house to keep her company, doing our homework until her father was home. It was late summer; the air was sticky and sweltering. All the window curtains were drawn, making it hard to tell whether it was evening or daylight. All we had to work by was a dim fan-shaped lamp shade hanging over that square dinner table in the living room. In this twilight a shadow in white drifted quietly by us.

That was Rong's mother. Her body was shrouded in a doctor's white gown, her face covered with a surgical mask, revealing only her eyes, which were staring straight ahead of her, stone-like and lifeless. All the time I was with Rong, her mother paced evenly back and forth between the kitchen and the living room. She never talked to me nor looked at me or at her daughter. Rong told me that she would walk like that all day long, except at dinner and bedtime, always wearing her doctor's gown and that mask. Never talking. Her arms crossed so her hands clutched her shoulders as if she were embracing herself. Her white gown billowed out, fluttering behind her, which made her appear to be hovering or drifting through water, like a ghost whose voice was frozen in the unbreakable ice of silence.

Watching Rong's mother and the art teacher and listening to their voices—wen or wu fengzi, either wild or silent—I felt my heart grow older, my gaze become weary, my vision harder and darker. Yet on one of those gray and gloomy summer afternoons when my grandmother first warned us about these crazed beings, I heard a different kind of voice, a voice that didn't fit either of the categories of wen or wu. It was neither wild nor silent; it was like a singing bird alighting on a leafless tree in a snowy winter, its tune resonating at once the chill of the winter and warmth of the spring.

In the summer of 1969, the Cultural Revolution entered its third year. The country was still burning with a giant firestorm, through which everyone's loyalty to Chairman Mao and the Party was put to the test. No one wanted to be burned to ashes and everyone wanted to prove themselves to be golden-hearted. Like everywhere else in the nation, our city had also turned into a battlefield where every day different revolutionary cells of Red Rebels and "conservatives" were fighting each other, accusing the other side of disloyalty.

Our residence complex, where the majority of the city's artists lived who were the central targets of this revolution, became one such battlefield. Both inside and outside the main entrance, the walls were covered with big-character posters. All the posters were filled with vehement and vicious words such as "Deep-fry those current antirevolutionaries!" "Burn alive those bourgeois reactionary literati!"

"If they don't surrender to the people, we will destroy them!"

"We must overthrow these reactionary intellectuals, beat them to the ground, and trample on them, so that they will never stand up again!"

My father's and his fellow black intellectuals' names were written upside down, with an *X* dripping with red and black ink; their features were caricatured in absurd distortions—as animals, such as a snake sneaking out of its lair and injecting poisonous saliva into a flowing river, or a crippled dog with a drooling tongue, foaming at the mouth, barking fiercely, at the shining red sun.

And along with these written invectives, there were verbal ones—daily mass meetings, street parades and group gatherings for verbal denunciations and attacks. On each side of the entrance to our complex were two square granite flower terraces, like two miniature gardens where various flowers had once grown and bloomed. With all the flowers gone, stomped on or pulled out, the terraces now became two small convenient stages on which every day the various revolutionary rebels gathered, denouncing vigorously our parents who were accused of using their pens to engage in antirevolutionary activities. During these oral battles, the accusers always opened their little red books, citing Mao's words, brandishing frantically their arms wrapped with red bands, shouting slogans and singing in high-pitched voices that made one's eardrum reverberate. Whenever we passed by the flower terraces into the complex, we felt such a shame that we hurried through the entrance as quietly and as quickly as possible, our heads down, for fear of drawing any attention.

On one summer afternoon returning from school, I was surprised to see that both terraces were free of any fanatic rebels. Instead, a man was standing on the flower terrace on the right; his calm and soft voice echoed above the unusually quiet crowd through the heat wave of the July air.

The man was in his late twenties or early thirties, about six feet tall, with a straight back and long legs. He wore a faded blue long-sleeve shirt and dark blue pants stained with dirt. His large deep-set brown eyes sparkled from beneath his bushy eyebrows; his dark skin was shadowed by his stubbly beard that merged with his sideburns into his thick ruffled black wavy hair, reaching almost to his shoulders. I was stunned. Nobody would dare to keep long hair now—it was considered a "decadent bourgeois" style. All citizens made the utmost effort to show their revolutionary loyalty both inside and out, including their wardrobe and hairstyles, which were regarded as the exterior signs of one's soul. To make sure one's exterior precisely reflects one's interior, one had to be extremely careful with his or her appearance. For both men and women, the basic principle for this dress code reflected the idea that a revolutionary should live a simple and plain life. Hence, while men wore a Mao jacket and women a double-breasted Lenin outfit either in black or blue, people followed a similar principle about their hairdo as well— simple and short. Girls and women sometimes could braid their hair or tie it into two short brushes (since wavy permed hair was regarded as a Western and bourgeois style); men without exception kept pingtou—a crew cut.

How bold this man must be: to keep that hairstyle that would remind everyone immediately of the "foreign ghosts" seen from caricatures on the big posters. His dark skin, deep-set eyes, and high-ridged nose made him look even more like one of those ghosts. But this ghost, in his mesmerizing voice, was singing. His sonorous voice, rising and falling as if on a tide, flew through the heated air like silver moonlight.

> I loved you once, nor can this heart be quiet,
> For it would seem that love still lingers here;
> But do not you be further troubled by it:
> I would in no wise sadden you, my dear.

I was transfixed, as much by his voice as by the song itself. Although I couldn't recall the tune, I did recognize the lyrics, a poem by Pushkin. I had heard my oldest sister and her friends reciting this and other poems by him.

I looked around nervously, my heart bouncing up and down. I almost could hear its drum-like beating. This man was doomed, I thought. To sing a love song like this in public was nothing short of committing suicide, not to mention that it was a poem by a Western poet. Within minutes, I knew, someone in the audience would charge toward him, seize the collar of his shirt and turn him into authority for this "offensive criminal activity."

Yet, nothing happened. No one made a move, except for a few teenagers who were giggling and cursing. Most of the audience was quiet, staring at the man as if he were not real, merely a ghost who had emerged from nowhere on this sweltering July afternoon. Then all of sudden, someone shot at his face with a slingshot. He didn't even dodge it, only rubbed on his instantly red and swollen left cheek and continued his singing, his eyes looking straight ahead cross the crowd, his arms reaching out into air as if trying to catch the raindrops falling from the sky.

Then I heard somebody whispering in the crowd, "He is a fengzi, a crazy man."

Later that evening, everyone in our complex was talking about this strange crazy man, yet no one really knew anything about him, except that he was a fengzi, whose family name was Wei. From then on, whenever we were back from school, about four or five o'clock in the afternoon, he would be there, sitting, standing, or squatting on one of the flower terraces. He seemed particularly fond of this small stage where he would recite poems, deliver Mao's speeches and poems, and sing the songs adapted to these speeches and poems called yuluge. I was amazed to hear how different a tone he used to sing the yuluge. It was true that every one of us in the crowd, literate or illiterate, could recite some of Mao's poems or words and sing those yuluge. Like wearing Mao buttons on the left side of one's chest, carrying around Mao's little red book, performing the Loyalty Dance, or chanting "Long live Chairman Mao," singing Mao's poems and sayings was just another revolutionary practice that could magically reveal our loyal hearts and protect us from any possible vicious attacks or accusations. These songs were usually performed to a nerve-shattering and hair-raising belligerent tune. It was rare to hear anyone sing Mao's sayings, or any other songs, in such a soft and soothing voice.

Being taught from an early age that our highest goal was to carry on the torch of the Communist revolution, we understood clearly that there were certain kind of songs that were not appropriate for us to listen to: those bad songs about love, for example. We were always warned against any of those "soft-tuned and decadent " songs that would make us captives of our own emotions and destroy our revolutionary spirit. Everyday, inside and outside school, loudspeakers installed within everyone's hearing range blasted out fierce and metallic music: "Three Main Rules of Discipline and Eight Points for Attention," "Sailing Depends on the Helmsman," "Internationale," "The East is Red," and of course, the eight revolutionary operas promoted by Madame Mao, Jiang Qing. Bombarded by these straining high-pitched notes, our ears were slowly going deaf to any other music that didn't sound revolutionary.

To me, those other tunes—those "nonrevolutionary" songs and music—comprised an important part of my happy early childhood. My parents used to have a huge collection of records, operas, and folk music. Stored in a three-layer red wooden case made by my grandfather, they were once the major source of entertainment for the whole family. Many chilly winter nights, when the north wind rattled the glass windows and snowflakes fell silently from the darkening sky, we all sat around the stove's shimmering coal fire, warming our hands and feet, listening to one record after another. Each of us had our own preferred music: my mother liked the folk songs and opera selections, my father enjoyed the soundtracks of his favorite old movies, and we preferred children's songs. I always volunteered to find a record for everyone. Holding its edge with my thumb and grabbing the hole with my middle finger, I put the record down on the rubber mat of the turntable, then lifted up the arm of the needle carefully as if I were holding a bird or a rosebud, and let it fall gently on the smooth and shining black surface of the record. Then I listened to the bird singing from that black forest and watched the rose bloom on a boundless plain of silent land.

But the bird would soon fly away and the rose wither. Those songs and music, like everything produced during the prerevolutionary era, became a poisonous legacy of the past that must be destroyed. The wooden case now sat in the inmost corner underneath my parents' bed, collecting dust. Spiderwebs sealed the passage from which birds once sang and roses bloomed.

Now Wei Fengzi's singing opened the door to that passage long closed to me.

One afternoon, I was late coming home. It was almost dusk. Several people were standing in front of a big-character poster, reading. I hurried toward the main entrance and saw Wei Fengzi sitting on the flower terrace, humming a melancholy tune. The song sounded very familiar, but I couldn't recall where I had ever heard it. I slowed down and waved to him; he didn't even notice me, still singing.

> The prairie is boundless and vast,
> I cannot see the end in sight.
> Please, my kind-hearted fellow,
> Would you take this ring with you?
> Please give it to the girl I love,
> Tell her I won't able to make it home . . .

While he was singing, Wei stared in front of him without looking at anybody. His body leaned forward; his arms reached out as if trying to grab hold of something or someone. Then he gradually withdrew his hands and put them on his shoulders, his eyes glistening with tears.

I shuddered and quickened my steps, suddenly anxious to go home. But the song and its doleful tune haunted me like a silent stream running toward the setting sun. I could feel its painful tenderness but was unable to catch up with its flow.

The house was quiet. My sisters and brother had gone out to play. My grandmother was getting supper. She added a few more pieces of coal into the stove and used a long iron hook to stir the embers to get rid of the gray ashes, which raised a mist of dust around the stove. She coughed a little, but continued poking the newly added coal to adjust them into proper position. Her hands were stained with gray and black coal dust.

I handed her a dust pan for her to scoop out those leftover ashes, then took it out and dumped in the trash bin. She then washed her hands and sat down beside the dinner table for a short break. I didn't want to waste any time.

"Nainai, do you know Wei Fengzi?"

"I know. You kids talk about this crazy man all the time."

"He is so different from other fengzi. Is he really one?"

"Of course, look at his eyes, look at his face. You stay away from him." My grandma looked and sounded somber.

"But," I hesitated, for a moment, "but he can sing. I like to hear him singing."

At this, my grandmother turned around and looked squarely at me. "What kind of songs he was singing? All bad ones, I'd say."

"Well, maybe, but those songs are so different, so sad, especially today." I described the words to my grandma and even tried to repeat the tune as much as I could, hoping to give her some clues. My grandma listened quietly and then nodded.

"That is a Russian folk song. It's about a horse carriage driver who lost his way in the Siberian steppes. Starving and thirsty, he knew he wouldn't be able to return home alive. So he took his engagement ring off his finger and begged the passersby to give it back to his fiancée waiting for him at his hometown. That was one of your mother's favorite songs. She has a good voice, your mother. She used to sing in the church choir. The momos there all loved listening to her sing."

"What? Church choir? Mama?" My limited knowledge of a church choir, gained from my father's storytelling, was associated with a romantic yet distant Western world. The idea that my mother had anything to do with it intrigued me. I knew mother liked singing and often heard her humming different tunes, whenever she was in a good mood. But she never told us about being in any singing group, not to mention a church choir.

I was about to push for more answers but my grandma, who seemed to have been taken aback by my questions, abruptly ended our conversation. She stood up and looked out at the window as if she were afraid somebody would eavesdrop. "Look at my babbling mouth. Your mother never told you, right? Now, go and get me some coal, quick, and by the way, you stay away from that Wei Fengzi. That is a strange, strange crazy man. You hear me?"

My grandma's warning was serious, but my desire to listen to Wei's singing was equally intense. Every day, when I came home, passing by the main entrance, Wei Fengzi was always there, standing on one of the flower terraces above the crowd, either chanting poems or singing songs. His deep and resonant voice always made me stop and listen. Now and then he would notice me and smile as he waved in my direction.

Sometimes in the late afternoon when we all came back from school, he would follow us into the complex, sit down at the edge of a square water fountain located in the middle of the yard, and continue his chanting and singing. We would gather around him, asking him to sing any songs we could think of—folk tunes, selections from operas—the songs we couldn't hear anywhere else—until the dusk fell and twilight darkened when our parents started calling us to come home for dinner. It was during these moments when we actually got a chance to talk to him. He was never offended and always took his time trying to answer our questions. Sometimes his narrative was coherent, although jumping here and there; other times, we found it difficult to follow his train of thought and were at a loss to understand his disjointed and garbled words.

From his fragmented memories and others' gossip, we gleaned that he used to be a so-called pre–Cultural Revolution college student, studying at Beijing University. He had been a well-rounded model student who made a name for himself in just about everything he did. But music was his biggest passion. While in school, he participated in a collegiate musical contest in Europe and won a silver medal. Along with it, he also won the heart of a young woman, one of his classmates and admirers.

When the Anti-Rightist Movement started in the early spring of 1957, his silver medal awarded by a Western musical competition and his outspoken passion for Western music raised suspicion and invited trouble. His girlfriend, who might have foreseen his doomed future, declared that she had cut off any tie with him. The fatal blow came, many believed, when she, to further demonstrate her loyalty to the Party, turned in all the love letters he once wrote to her to the school Party Committee. Some of these letters quoted a fair number of Western poets, which, of course, provided ample evidence of his disloyalty as a "walking dog of foreign devils."

He was later expelled from school and sent back to his birthplace, a small rural town in southern Anhui Province. What happened between then and now was anyone's guess. But eventually he wandered into Hefei, where he assumed a new identity as Wei Fengzi. No one knew for sure when and how this new identity started taking shape; no one knew for certain whether he was a real fengzi or a fake one. But to me, that didn't really matter. All I knew, and with deep gratitude, was that because of this mysterious stranger who was known to this world only as Wei Fongzi, I found my way back to a lost place where birds used to sing and roses bloomed.

As the summer was coming to an end and days were getting shorter and shorter, his presence was less and less frequent. The rumor had it that the city policemen turned their attention to him and began to restrict his whereabouts. It was believed that they would eventually force him to leave the city for his hometown. On a few occasions when he did appear he looked haggard and worn; his faded blue shirt was wrinkled and stained with mud and both his hair and beard grew longer. But his eyes didn't lose their sparkle, and he was still singing.

On an early autumn dusk, we were all home early, helping our grandma prepare supper. It was quiet outside. Children were all back home; no one was playing in the yard. Only the wind could be heard sweeping dry leaves off the trees and swirling them around with a loud whistle. Then, all of sudden, we heard that familiar voice. Through the window, I saw Wei Fengzi standing beside the water fountain. From his lonely silhouette a song flowed toward the dark orange and purple horizon. My sisters and I stopped setting up the table, approached the window, and listened. My grandma, who was busy cooking at the time, shook her head but didn't say anything.

Suddenly, I remembered the song. It was called "Song of Midnight," from an old movie with the same title. I had never seen the movie because all the movies produced before 1966 were banned. But more than once I had listened to the song on one of our records and heard the film's story from different sources.

It was a tragic love story set in the turmoil of the war-torn 1940s. A prominent young actor, Danping, fell in love with a beautiful girl Yun. But Yun's father, a rich and powerful man who wanted his daughter to marry into high society, forbade the marriage. To eliminate any possibility for the young lovers to be together, the father hired someone to disfigure Danping by pouring sulphuric acid on his face. Out of despair for both love and his career as an actor, Danping threw himself into a river, only to be saved by a passerby who helped him find a hiding place in the backstage of the theater where Danping had performed many plays in the past.

From then on, every midnight, people could hear a voice singing from the backstage of the theatre. The theater, which many now believed to be haunted by a singing ghost, was soon deserted. Twenty-seven years later, an aged Yun who had never married learned from a mutual friend that Danping was still alive and that the ghost haunting the theater was none other than the very man she had been dreaming about for the past twenty-seven years. She pleaded with her friend to take her to see him. But Danping vehemently refused, horrified at the thought of letting her see his face. Not deterred by this rejection and determined to be with Danping, Yun removed the last obstacle by blinding herself with a needle. With the help of their friend, Yun and Danping finally met at the backstage of the theater where they never left each other's arms again. Not long after that, on a quiet summer's eve at midnight, a fierce fire broke out and engulfed the entire theater. Danping and Yun never appeared afterward. The song Wei Fengzi was singing now was the one Danping sang from the backstage of the theater for twenty-seven years as a ghost.

We listened and watched him through the frosted windowpane. The sun descended from the sky, hanging pale like a sickle above the tree line that swayed along with the rhythm of his voice. The darkening sky pressed upon his head like a floating shadow that was about to bury him. As if unable to bear its weight, he sank to his knees, his shoulders drooping, his arms wrapped around his chest like a wounded bird holding its wings, ready to fly, not with its wings, but with the flow of the wind.

That was the last time I saw Wei Fengzi and listened to his songs.

After that night, Wei Fengzi never returned. He had flown away like a singing bird into a dark forest, leaving behind a faint rhythm that crashed a silver line across the overcast sky, a rhythm that was as strong as dream, as beautiful as hope.

Every now and then, in a deep quiet night, I imagine I can still hear him singing songs and chanting poems, just as I can hear the chilling wail from the demented art teacher and the haunting silence from Rong's ghost-like mother. All these different voices of the winds have folded into one another until I can now hardly tell which is which. These voices, each in its own way, have helped shape and strengthen the voice of my own wind.

槐花 *6*

The Song of the Golden Phoenix

On the wall of my father's study hangs a wood-framed black-and-white photo of four young men and women, standing side by side on the stone stairs in front of a golden-shingled dark red granite building. Under its golden roof is a horizontal board inscribed with five cursive characters that read "Jianghuai Grand Theater." The woman second on the left wears a floral-patterned short-sleeve shirt and a knee-length skirt; the man to her left wears a green army uniform. The woman on the far right, who wears a longer skirt, is leaning against a tall man in a plain white shirt with his sleeves rolled up. It must have been a sunny day because their eyes are all squinting a little under the dazzling sunlight. Their young and vivacious faces radiate smiles toward the camera.

In the winter of 2004, during our stay in my parents' home, my six-year-old daughter Anying seemed to be particularly curious about this photo and asked me who these people were. When I told her the couple on the right were her grandparents, her eyes were wide open as she exclaimed, "Wow, they are so young!!!"

The other couple, I told her, the woman in the short floral shirt and skirt and the man in the army uniform, were her grandparents' best friends. The woman was an opera actress named Fongying, meaning a brave and a beautiful phoenix. The man beside her was her husband, Gong Ge, a drama director.

"Where are they now? Are they still Yeiyei and Nainai's friends? Can I get to meet them?"

"Yes, they are still their friends. Nothing will ever change that. But you won't get to see them."

"Why?"

Why? Confronted by her curious eyes, for a moment I couldn't find a good answer to this simple question. I could have said that woman is now dead; she died not long after that picture was taken, when she was at the age of thirty-five. The man is still alive, although no one is certain of that since he seems to have disappeared altogether from the eyes of the world. But I knew that no matter how I tried to explain, my words wouldn't make much sense to her. The truth is, there are no easy answers. When my father brought together these two close friends of his into what many believed to be a heavenly match, he couldn't anticipate, of course, years later, that this perfect match would be broken by the untimely and unexpected death of one and the insanity of the other. He would spend many sleepless nights afterward trying to figure out what had caused this end and why it happened the way it did. My father was never able to reach the conclusion, as others did, of pointing a finger toward the husband. Was he truly a coward as many people believed? If he could have known the consequence of his action, would he have done things differently? And if he had indeed done things differently, could he have saved his wife's life? And later his own sanity?

I know I may not be able to tell the story to my child in such a way that she could comprehend. But I will try. It is never too early or too late to talk and to listen.

For the majority of Chinese intellectuals who initially were attracted to and inspired by the Communist idealism of building a utopian society in which people lived in perfect harmony with one another and enjoyed mutual respect and individual dignity, the early years after the establishment of the young republic swelled with hopes and dreams. Like many other intellectuals of his time, my father embraced whole-heartedly the Communist Party which, he believed, would lead the country into an unprecedented prosperity and strength, leaving behind the oppression, humiliation, deprivation, poverty, chaos, backwardness, corruption, and dictatorship that had plagued the nation for hundreds and hundreds of years. Such hopes, dreams, faith, and enthusiasm brought forward a brief period of flourishing literary creation in the history of the young republic between 1950 and 1956.

In the early 1950s when he was in his late twenties, my father won his very first national literary award for a one-act play entitled *Home Coming*. It was a story about a village woman who refused to subject herself to the fate of an abandoned wife and eventually took control of her life. Its success sparked my father's interest in contemporary drama, especially Huangmei Xi, a major regional opera, a genre that combined a variety of forms such as speaking, dancing, and singing, in addition to acting. He frequently visited the Huangmei theater and befriended many actors and directors. Among them was Aunt Fongying, the leading actress of the provincial Huangmei Opera Troupe.

To me, Aunt Fongying was the dear aunt I never had. Each of my parents had a younger sister, but both died as infants. Aunt Fongying seemed to be the reincarnation of these two aunts who hadn't able to live beyond their first year. She was tall and slim, had a perfectly shaped oval face, a straight-ridged nose, and thick eyelashes covering her deep curved eyes that seemed to be smiling all the time. She addressed my father and my mother respectively as dage (big brother) and saozi (sister-in-law) and my grandma as "mama." She would come to our house at least once a week, sometimes with her husband Uncle Gong, a tall, handsome man who was always dressed in a faded army uniform, and their two sons. Each time, she would bring various small gifts she had made herself: a necklace of freshwater pearls, a tiny elegant purse made of bright colored plastic ribbons, a red wax paper lantern, a small cloth doll she had sewn and then painted. The best part of her visit was always her singing, and sometimes even dancing. As we watched her swirl around and listened to her sugary mellow voice, we were spellbound as if by a beautiful heavenly fairy who flew down from Heaven to this earthly world, touching us mortals with her immortal magic power. We would plead with her to sing one song after another, until our parents came to her rescue.

My mother, who also loved singing, often joined Aunt Fongying, sometimes even practicing a few steps or gestures after her; then they would tease each other, giggling like two young girls. From my mother I learned a lot about Aunt Fongying, who was only seven when her parents died of famine. One of her distant uncles adopted her and sent her the same year to the local Huangmei theatrical troupe as an apprentice to become an actress. It was an occupation many poor families had chosen for their girls as a way of relieving financial burdens. Once signed away to a troupe by their parents, these young girls could no longer control their fate and were subjected to various physical and mental abuses, either from the troupes or other forces. When Aunt Fongying was about sixteen and had just started making a name for herself by singing and acting in the region, one official in the service of a local warlord noticed her while watching her play. He ordered the head of the opera troupe to have Fongying sent to him right away as one of his concubines. Aunt Fongying managed to escape from the troupe and went to Nanjing, a big city in Jiangsu province where she later joined a local opera troupe that belonged to the People's Liberation Army.

In spring of 1950, after the Communist Party won the civil wars against the Nationalist Party and established the People's Republic, Aunt Fongying returned to Anhui province and later became the leading actress in the provincial Huangmei Opera Troupe. By staging traditional plays such as *Match of Heaven*, *Female Prince*, and *Lantern Festival* and having all of them adapted into movies which were then shown nationwide, Aunt Fongying helped revitalize and draw national attention to the regional Huangmei opera. But she had a bigger dream for its future. She believed that it was time for the Huangmei opera to step beyond traditional themes

and venture into a new era. She discussed this idea with my father
and asked him if he would write a script with a contemporary
theme. It was true that my father had written several plays, but most
of them were spoken dramas, like his award-winning one-act play. A
script for a Humangmei opera was something new since it involved
speaking, singing, and dancing. Also, he was then focusing on fiction
writing and movie scripts. But my father didn't hesitate and was
actually glad to have this opportunity to create something new for
Aunt Fongying.

Three months later, he finished a new script entitled *The Song
of the Golden Phoenix*. It was about a young village girl who was sold
by her poor parents as a child bride. When she grew up, she refused
to marry the man she had been betrothed to, a man she regarded as
her own brother. The whole village then turned against her, treating
her as if she were a witch who would bring ill fate to the village if
she indeed broke the tradition. But she wouldn't be forced into sub-
mission. Her sheer determination to control her life eventually won
her the respect and support of her fiancé—her step brother—who
helped her reunite with the love of her own choice.

Aunt Fongying told my mother that every time she read the
script, she couldn't hold back her tears; it reminded her so much of
her own past, how she fought her own battles to win her freedom.
She couldn't wait, she said, to work on the play. But the first thing
was to find a director who was willing to take a risk with the contemporary theme in traditional Humanmei Opera. They didn't need
to go far—my father thought of Uncle Gong. They had known each
other back in high school years. When they graduated, my father
went to the city to work for the army as a civilian, while Uncle Gong
joined the Liberation Army and later became a director in the Gen-
eral Army Drama Opera. At the time he was just about to be transferred from the Army Opera Troupe to the Anhui region. Staging
Aunt Fongying's play would be a perfect opportunity for this young,
energetic, and ambitious director. By inviting him to direct the play,
my parents also indulged a small secret wish. Both thought Aunt
Fongying and Uncle Gong were a born match, lacking only an

opportunity to be brought together. The play, then, functioned as a matchmaker to some extent.

My parents' secret wish soon became a reality. Aunt Fongying and Uncle Gong, like two shooting stars, fell into each other's sky and neither wanted to leave ever after. What followed was natural, as my father described it, like a "floating cloud and flowing water," a culmination for what many people saw as "a heavenly match." The play was staged in the early spring of 1955 and became a huge success. Two months later Aunt Fongying and Uncle Gong got married. During the next three years Aunt Fongying and Uncle Gong had two sons who would later become our good friends and playmates. Sometimes, when we were bored with our own games, Aunt Fongying and Uncle Gong would perform their antiphonal song and dance to entertain us. One of my favorites was a snatch from the opera *The Match of Heaven* when the beautiful seventh daughter of the Celestial Queen Mother, who fell in love with a poor but good-natured peasant, Dongyong, was leaving the Palace of Heaven to start a new life on earth.

Their performance not only brought us children joy and fun, but was also a much-expected entertainment in many adult gatherings in our house. During the relatively peaceful time before 1966, our house was frequented by a glittering company of literary guests—novelists, poets, actors, critics, journalists, photographers, and literary translators. Many of them, my father included, were members of the Communist Party who genuinely believed that their life goal, as the Party said, was to establish a harmonious world in which freedom and democracy would prevail. With this belief and hope, these enthusiastic and energetic young intellectuals (mostly in their early thirties) often had lively debates in our living room—fierce yet friendly battles in which they eloquently discussed many issues that needed to be addressed in order to build a new and more prosperous future for the young republic.

Unlike most Chinese parents who always ordered their children away from adult gatherings, my father let us stay if we wanted to. He thought it would be educational for us even just sitting there to listen and feel the passionate conversations and debates. My brother and I used to pull out our small stools and sit quietly in the corner, leaning our backs against the wall, watching and listening for hours and hours. Although too young to understand what they said, the way they engaged in their discussion—telling stories, cracking jokes, chanting poems, singing songs, sometimes even acting, glued us to where we sat from the beginning to the end.

But not long after, the vibrant and enchanting voices of these young men and women would be silenced for years to come. What enabled them to dismiss the potential danger and encouraged them to speak out and express concerns—their passion for the future of the nation, their insatiable intellectual curiosity and pursuit of human knowledge—would, ironically, relegate them to the lowest rung of the society—"stinking No. 9s, " a special term given to the intellectuals. Many of them would later be subjected to a prolonged mental and physical torture, including labor camp, jail, and ultimately, death.

The news of Aunt Fongying's death arrived among the earliest reports. Between 1966 and 1967 when the Cultural Revolution stormed the nation and hit every corner of the land, Aunt Fongying had become the first target picked from the Provincial Opera Troupe. All the big-character posters attacked her as a principal figure of the old feudalist tradition of Huangmei opera. She went through endless sessions of self-criticism and confession and was regularly hauled out for the mass denunciation meetings and street parades. But every now and then she still managed to visit us in the midst of all that chaos. When she did come, my mother and grandmother would sit with her around the big dinner table, sometimes whispering to one another, but most of the time silent. My father had by then been sent to the secluded "reform camp" outside the city, coming home only once a month. He and Aunt Fongying rarely had the chance to see each other.

I remember the last time Aunt Fongying came was on a Saturday evening in the early summer of 1968. She wanted to see my father, who was expected to return home that weekend. I was already in bed, but so worried about my father, I couldn't fall asleep. I heard Aunt Fongying whisper to my grandma, asking if she could wait a while. It was not until late in the night when I heard a squeak of our front door and my father's heavy steps. His tall lanky shadow flashed for a second in the door frame of our bedroom and disappeared. I then heard him clear and lower his voice.

"Are you . . . all right? For now?"

Aunt Fongying whispered back, "I am fine. What about you?" A huskiness crept into her voice and was followed by a sigh, as when dusk fell.

"Me?" my father responded with another sigh. "What about me? Just to pass each day. That's all. Every day counts. You never know what it will be like tomorrow."

"Yeah, tomorrow." Aunt Fongying's voice lifted up a little.

"How is Gong Ge?"

"He is fine—busy, though." Her voice turned low again.

Then I heard my grandmother sigh. "Listen to me, Fongying. You must get through this. You can never do anything silly, all right?"

Aunt Fongying coughed dryly. "Don't worry. I will be fine. Yanzhou and I have to work on another play, don't we?"

"What?" my father sounded as if he had been just awakened from sleep.

"Don't you remember? You promised me you would write another play. I haven't forgotten. I will be waiting for that day."

My father recounted this conversation in an essay he wrote ten years after Aunt Fongying's death.

"Here we are," he recalled, "two prisoners who are temporarily out of jail, uncertain what will be waiting for us tomorrow, which for all we know, will be another day of torture, denunciations, forced confession, and humiliations. No one was even sure if we could survive another tomorrow. And here she is, discussing the possibility of us working on another Huangmei opera—the heart and soul of her life. I looked at her and felt so ashamed of myself, having already given up on the idea of ever writing again. Her eyes, smiling at me, were like sparkling stars, stars that lit up the dark night which I now know will see its end, sooner or later."

But that star fell not long after that dusk night ended.

About three months after that Saturday visit, Aunt Fongying died, on an autumn day in 1968, from an overdose of sleeping pills. She was pronounced dead on arrival at the hospital. By that time, like other young kids I had heard of or witnessed many suicide attempts—attempts made through slashing arteries with a razor, hanging from a door frame, or jumping out of buildings—and was almost beyond feeling any shock or sorrow at those lost lives. But Aunt Fongying's death struck me hard. I found it difficult to understand how a fairy like her could actually die, and moreover, how she could die from an overdose of sleeping pills.

To my young mind, among all the chosen methods of death, taking sleeping pills had the minimum possibility of success. At least three adults in our complex—two women writers and one poet—chose to take pills but all survived. Aunt Li Na, one of the women writers and a close friend of my father's, took two bottles of sleeping pills one night but found herself still alive the next morning, although suffering terrible pain. She somehow managed to ask for help and got it from those living next door. Along with other children, I pushed through the crowd into the room where she lay on the cold hardwood floor of her apartment. Beside her were a water basin, a tube, and soap; several adults were trying to pour soapy water down her throat which, it was believed, could make her vomit and wash the pills out of her stomach. Her body, dressed in black silk shirt and pants, twisted back and forth in agony, accompanied by sporadic groans and screams. I was only a few inches away from her and could see clearly her pale face, tightly closed eyes, tangled wet hair and naked wrinkled feet. I could have been looking at a corpse, only I knew that those feet would start walking again.

Not Aunt Fongying, who didn't make her way back to us.

Her absence was soon filled by a shadowy and shaking figure. It was her husband, Uncle Gong, the young, handsome, and ambitious theater director. One dark evening in the late fall, about three months after Aunt Fongying's death, he showed up at our house. His body seemed to have shrunk to half of its original size while his face looked double his age. His hair was disheveled, already turning gray. The wrinkles on his jaw were so tight that they seemed about to explode. His steps were uncertain and hesitant, like a lonely and crippled traveler who wandered on a strange path while glancing nervously around as if expecting the sudden fearful appearance of a ghost.

My parents were not home: my father had been sent to the labor camp and my mother assigned to the rural area about a hundred miles away from the city. Uncle Gong sat on one side of our dinner table, while my grandma, on the other side, was sewing shoes; neither of them talked. Hours later, he got up and left.

That was the first of many subsequent nights when Uncle Gong would visit and sit, mostly in silence, with my grandma. Occasionally, he would break the silence and mumble a few words, most often like, "It was all my fault, it was my fault . . ."

He would keep saying that over and over again until my grandma, who became visibly impatient, cut him short. "Of course, it was your fault. But what is the use to say it now, huh? You cannot bring Fongying back, can you?"

My grandma was stitching the sole of a black cloth shoe. She drew back and forth a long thick linen thread through the sole with a loud swishing sound.

At these words, Uncle Gong covered his face with his hands as if afraid that my grandma would whip him with her flaxen thread. "No, I can't. But how I wish I had done it differently."

"Too late then." My grandma let out a deep sigh. "You have to take good care of yourself. For the kids' sake."

"They hate me now. They think their mother died because of me. And they are right. It was me who killed Fongying."

"Don't say that." My grandma frowned to show that she was irritated.

"Yes, it was me, it was me . . ."

My grandmother lost her patience, stood up, tossed away her sewing, and exploded: "Yes, it was you! Of course it was you! If it were not for you, Fongying would still be alive. Yes, it was your fault. But what can you do now? For heaven's sake, be a man for your sons!"

Uncle Gong seemed stunned, his mouth hanging open, his eyes staring blankly at nothing in particular. It took a solid five minutes before he picked up words again.

"Ma, you are right. I have sons to take care of. I must . . ." He choked with his words, slowly rose from the chair, and staggered out of the room. The darkness swallowed his shadow and closed its heavy door behind him.

I too was shocked by my grandmother's explosion of anger. I had never seen or even known this side of her. When she turned around and saw me, my grandma took me in her arms, gently stroked my hair, and spoke in a much softened voice.

"I didn't mean to frighten you, Sanzi. I cannot stand that coward husband! He is the only one who could have saved your Aunt Fongying. But what is the use now? Too late, too late . . ."

My grandmother's voice was drawn in a gust of whistling wind. It was the late autumn. I could hear the wind sweeping the leaves off the phoenix tree in front of our house and imagined how its almost naked branches were shivering in the chilled air.

I was shivering too as I listened to a familiar yet strange voice singing from the phoenix tree in the darkness outside.

Finally, she let out a long, deep sigh of relief, lay down on the double bed, closed her eyes, and waited.

How long would it take for her to go? An hour? Longer? Through the window, she could see that the leaves of the phoenix trees by the balcony were almost gone. How come they went so fast? Every spring until early fall, these leaves would provide a green canopy over their third-floor balcony, streams of sunlight filtering through this canopy of leaves, casting tiny pieces of glittering diamonds that danced along with the swing of the gentle spring breeze.

But the leaves were all gone now. That deep forest green. Those sparkling sun diamonds. They would be back. Next spring. Only she would be long gone by then and unable to see. By the time her husband

and two sons returned home, she would have left for another world, where she could finally have a moment of peace. She would not be forced to her knees again, while those revolutionary rebels screamed insults, punching and kicking her. She wouldn't have to write those endless self-criticisms and confessions. How many had she written? She couldn't even remember. But they were never good enough. Tonight, there would be another mass meeting when she was expected to give yet another self-denunciation speech. But she wouldn't be there. The very thought of it gave her a tinge of relief. No more torture and humiliation. It was almost time to go. She felt her body was sinking down each day and her limbs were gradually turning numb. Recently, she had begun seeing and hearing some strange things. She kept seeing the phoenix tree leaves resplendent in the sun and hearing the sound of someone singing, faint and sweet, accompanied by thousands of distant Chinese violins.

That is the Seventh Fairy singing to me, she once said to her husband. He gave her a fearful and stern look, telling her to stop such nonsense.

But she forgot or didn't know how to stop. She told him about many dreams she had, in one of which she said, "You and I were on the stage and the lights were on. But when we were about to perform, the lights went out and you disappeared. I was dancing alone in the dark, waiting for you to return to me. Then I fell asleep on the stage. The next morning when I woke up, I couldn't see. I didn't have eyes anymore. I had holes instead."

He again demanded that she stop. He was so angry, and she felt terrible to upset him that much.

Well, I won't be bothering him for long. Hope there isn't too much pain. Thank heaven I have saved these magic pills. What would I do without them? Yes, I could jump from the balcony or slash my wrists. But no, I can't let him and my sons remember me as a ghastly-looking ghost with blood all over my body. This way, they will think I just fell into a long sleep and won't be as scared.

Her eyes fell on the cream-colored silk blouse and skirt she was wearing; a smile flashed through her face. It was reassuring to put on her favorite dress, the only one she had rescued from being burned by hiding it at the bottom of her old wooden trunk. It was all wrinkled now and its cream had turned brownish, some of the buttons lost. But it didn't matter. It was hers.

Then she remembered something. It suddenly occurred to her that she had forgotten one more touch—to put on some makeup. She struggled to sit up, got off the bed, inched toward the oak dresser, and sat down in front of the oval mirror. How many times had she sat here, mornings and evenings, and put on her foundation, powder, rouge, and finally the lipstick before combing her hair? As she held out her right hand trying to reach for something, she saw that the surface was now empty of any bottles or boxes. She hadn't put on makeup since two years ago, when all her accessories—powders, lipstick, rouge, and jewelry—were either lost or destroyed.

But she had to take a final look at her face, to make sure it was not ghost-like and would not scare her young children. She strained her eyes and looked into the mirror but could see only a shadow shaking in pure whiteness. She felt tired, her chest constricting. A chilly wave surged over her, like someone was pouring icy cold water over her body. She opened her eyes, but couldn't see anything. Then she remembered that dream. Instead of eyes, she had holes. And into these holes she was falling, her head spinning and body swirling, faster and faster down into that pitch dark bottom when she heard a loud and shrill scream, a terrifying and terrified scream that struck her like a clap of thunder:

"Help! Help!"

She was wide awake now and her chest flooded with horror. What have I done? What about my two boys, what about him? Would it only make matters worse if I am gone? My good heaven, how selfish I am! How can I just think about myself? What will this house be like without a woman? Would they be spared all the troubles or given more, because of what I have done?

But, but, do I still have time? Or is it too late?

She turned her stiff neck toward the white square wall clock, its black minute and hour hands turning into a straight line, like a solitary tree frozen in a field of snow. It was eleven thirty. In about half an hour both boys would be back. It would be lunch time. She struggled to her feet; a wave of dizziness almost swept her off balance. Staggering and shivering, *she felt her way back to her bed; once she reached its edge, she grabbed the wooden headboard to prevent herself from falling.*

What should I do now? Do I still have time to do it?

Then she heard the door knob turning. A small figure squeezed through the door, leaving it ajar, through the opening she saw the dim-lighted corridor looming like a deep and dark cave.

"Xiao?"

"Yes, Mama?" The boy was startled.

"Where is your brother?"

"He went to his friends'. Back soon."

The boy looked at his mother with concern, wondering why she was sitting up in bed during daytime instead of cooking.

"Are you all right? Mama? Are you sick or something?"

"Xiao."

"Yes?"

"Listen to me. Mama asks you a favor, a big favor."

The boy became quiet, listening to his mother attentively. His big black eyes blinked with uncertainty.

"I am not feeling well. Actually, very, very sick. Could you go get your father?"

"Isn't he at the meeting right now?"

"Yes, please, get him as soon as you can."

"Can I first play a little while?"

"No, you cannot wait. Mama may not have that much time."

"What do you mean? I don't have to go back to school until two o'clock."

"I need you to get your father right now. I need him."

The boy mumbled, a little upset, but obeyed and went out.

The hands on the wall clock started drifting apart; the lonely tree split into two, one half moving forward while the other stayed put.

Unable to sit for long, she lay down flat on her back. It was cold. She tried to pull up the quilt up to her neck, but the quilt felt like a tube full of lead. One minute her heart was burning with fire and the next it was frozen with ice.

Please, let the boy find him. I need him; I must tell him the truth and ask him for his forgiveness. We may still have time. But what would the doctors say? I can tell them that I took a wrong bottle. Oh, would they believe me? I cannot think about that now. My head hurts so much, so does my chest. Everywhere. Like I am bleeding inside.

The door cracked open. She turned her head a bit, a small round face floating into the line of her vision. She tried to sit up.

"Hi, Mama."

"Yes? Where is . . . your . . . father?

"He is still in the meeting." He grumbled, his eyes cast down and shoulders drooping as if ashamed that he didn't accomplish what his mother told him to. "Baba said he couldn't leave in the middle of the meeting. He said it would only cause more trouble for you. He asked if you were working on your self-criticism for this evening's mass denunciation meeting."

She fell back into her bed. She opened her mouth but no words came out. She felt fire burning from underneath, its flame scorching her body and blurring her vision. *Maybe I don't need him, she thought. Did I take enough dosage? Maybe I will be fine after all.*

These thoughts were cut short by a sudden jerk of her body that was followed by a violent shake as if she were receiving an electric shot. She struggled out of the bed, once again, and moved her heavy legs one at a time, toward the sink. She heard that soap could help wash pills out of one's stomach. That small piece of transparent soap lying at the corner of the sink might be her only chance. She turned on the faucet which started dripping. On the third floor, the water was almost always trickling; often, there was none. Without waiting for the water, she grabbed that piece of soap and shoveled into her mouth and swallowed it down.

For a second, all her internal movement seem to have stopped. Then, within minutes, everything burst all over inside. Her entire body started shaking convulsively as if pushed from inside by a wild animal that was desperately fighting to get out. It could hardly wait for her to open mouth before it gushed out in yellowish and greenish liquid which splashed on the floor, again and again, until her stomach turned empty and numb. An odor of a mixture of soapy water and rotten fruit spread all over the room.

Her son, who was playing near the balcony door with his folded cig-arette wrappers, started screaming. He dashed out of the door and pounded with his little fists on the neighbor's door across the hallway.

She felt her body begin floating, as light as air, and then it fell soundlessly onto the cold cement floor. Neither her son's screaming nor the neighbors' panicked shouting could wake her up enough for her to move.

She didn't know how long it was before she heard a groan of the door.

Her husband's voice drifted into her ears, bringing close to her a face she now could hardly recognize.

"It is me, Fongying. It is me."

She turned her head toward the voice, and unable to talk, she lifted her finger and pointed to an empty bottle and then at her own stomach.

"You ate them all?" His eyes were bulging out a little, as if he had just cried.

She nodded, feeling nauseous again.

"Why? Are you out of your mind? They let you stay home so that you could prepare for this evening's . . ."

He stopped abruptly as if realizing how stupid the question was he had asked.

"Sorry," she mouthed. She could no longer utter any sound. Her voice, like everything else in her body, was slowly taking its leave.

"Hospital. Please, hospital." She gestured, first at her chest and at the door, or rather the direction of the door. She was losing her vision, too.

"How long ago did you take these pills?" He demanded; his eyes flashing with fear and despair.

She stared towards him, her eyeballs burning too. She could see a flame rising.

"How long, how long?" He became irritated.

She shook her head. Since this morning, she said. But no voice came out.

Why does that matter? Please, take me to the hospital. Please. The fire is burning inside me. My voice is gone, but my heartbeat hasn't stopped. I can hear it, I can feel it.

But he didn't hear her heartbeat. In fact, he couldn't hear or see anything. His mind, paralyzed and unable to form any coherent thoughts, was now functioning only in a shadow of fear: his wife, an alleged anti-Party actress who was expected to deliver yet another self-denouncement to the whole opera troupe that evening, had swallowed a bottle of sleeping pills. What do they call it? To resist revolution with suicide; to defy the Party and People with death.

What should I do now? I can't just go and take her to hospital. The Party secretary has to be informed first. I must report to him her situation first before taking her anywhere. Should I? That is my responsibility, right? I am a Party member. I can't just do what I want to do. But what about her?

I can now run to the auditorium. It will take about five minutes and I will have to wait for him to make a decision. Then what is next; no, no, ask him first. But she is my wife. I should do something right now. But what will happen to me, and to her? He kept punching his forehead; his eyes started seeing tiny golden stars. But he knew it was useless. He knew fully well that he might never be able to find a way out of this endless dark tunnel of thought.

Without realizing it, he had let go of his wife's hands, which like the rest of her body, had slipped away from him. He bent over toward her and pulled up the quilt and tucked it under her neck.

"Sorry, Fongying, wait for me. I will be right back. I promise you. We cannot afford to cause more troubles now. For both of us. I will be right back. It won't take long. Wait for me. Wait for me."

Then he hurried out of the door and disappeared. She could hear his heavy steps pounding on the stone stairways, hammering nails into her chest. But she didn't feel any pain. There was no need to fight any more. It wouldn't be of any use. It was over. She heaved a deep sigh of relief and closed her eyes. A warm darkness enveloped her. She started flying slowly toward the sky, like the Seventh Fairy.

The door was pushed open from outside. "Fongying, hold on. Hold on. I am here. The Party Secretary agreed. He said to send you to hospital first.

I borrowed a flatbed cart from the office. We are going to the hospital, right now. Do you hear me? We are going to the hospital."

She thought she had opened her eyes but remembered that they had now turned into holes through which she could see nothing. Her body was lifted up, carried through the dark corridor, down the narrow stairs, and onto a cart with two boards on each side. She felt a hand touching her hair and heard that familiar voice whispering: "Fongying, Fongying, don't leave me, don't leave us! We are on our way to the hospital . . . hospital . . . hospital . . ."

The voice slowly drifted away and joined the faint murmuring of thousands of Chinese violins she had once heard in a dream. She saw again those sparkling diamonds falling through the forest green canopy of phoenix tree leaves, striking haunting notes that echoed into the waiting darkness.

All is quiet now. What could have been said is forever left unsaid; what could have been done is forever left undone. Those two young faces can only look at us in silence, smiling from the wall. The madness of that distant era is long gone and the grand march is over, but when faced with the question of why, asked by those innocent and curious minds, we are not yet prepared to answer, either for them or ourselves. Time lost cannot be reversed and the lives destroyed can never be salvaged. But that is all the more reason for us to remember, for our own and our children's sakes.

So we must forever ask why and try to answer.

槐花 7

Fairyland

This is a story told to me by a xianren, an immortal, under an old willow tree beside a clear-bottomed pond on a beautiful sunny spring morning.

It was the spring of 1998, the year I returned to China with my six-month-old daughter for her first visit to my hometown. We stayed first at my parents' place in the west end of the city and then at my parents-in-law's in the south. My parents-in-law live on the campus of the provincial art school where my father-in-law has been teaching for the past thirty years. The school used to enjoy a reputation for nurturing many bright stars in the field of entertainment—actors, singers, and dancers—both inside and outside the province. Its campus on about one hundred acres is covered with plush green grass. In the middle is a small pond encircled by a row of willow trees. Farther east of the pond are several gray concrete dorms for both faculty and students, and at the west, about two hundred meters away from the pond, stands a six-story building of red bricks and a dark blue-shingled roof with a tower in the center and two wings on each side. A three-meter-wide concrete pathway circles the building like a motionless body of water.

During our weekly stay at my parents-in-law's, every morning shortly after sunrise, I would push the blue floral stroller where my daughter was snuggling and walk along the pond under the willow trees. It was very quiet on these spring mornings, when most students were still in bed. Every time I would see an old man who wore tang zhuang, a traditional white satin long-sleeved top and baggy pants, practice Chinese boxing and other martial arts movements under one of the biggest willow trees whose branches almost touched the water. He was in his late sixties or early seventies, medium height, strong build; an angular face with a furrowed forehead, a firm jutting chin, and deep-set eyes hidden beneath thick eyebrows. His gestures were graceful and focused. As he moved, his long white beard, which reached to his chest, fluttered slightly in the gentle breeze, as did his white satin shirt and pants. His body seemed to be floating off the ground and up in the sunlit air.

"That is a xianren. An immortal. Live forever," my father-in-law said, when I mentioned the old man to him. I almost burst into laughter, but quickly checked myself, seeing that he was not joking.

"That is what everybody says. He is a xianren. He once jumped out of that tower of our main building, like a bird flying downward, and landed right on that concrete road. Many people saw it. He didn't die. Didn't even get hurt. Isn't he a xianren, or what? Good heaven knows what saved him."

It was another sunny and warm spring morning when I saw the xianren again. I stood not far from him, my stroller parked right beside that willow tree he always practiced by. We made brief eye contact and both smiled. He then sauntered toward the stroller and looked closely at the baby inside.

"What a beautiful little girl!" He let out a sigh, his eyes glowing with the tenderness of the morning sunlight as his voice rolled over the grass like the sparkling beads of dew. Then he turned around and disappeared behind the willow tree trunk, only to reemerge in an instant with a willow branch in one hand and a small bunch of wildflowers in the other. With a speed and dexterity not usually seen in a man his age, he twisted his fingers back and forth, left and right, and up and down, in between the branch and the flowers. In no time, he finished weaving a willow crown decorated with twinkling stars of colorful flowers and handed it to me.

"She will like this; girls always like flowers." His wrinkled face blossomed into a sunny grin.

My baby, as if knowing a present was waiting for her, now woke up; her eyes opened wide, searching around. I waved the floral crown in front of her, and she started giggling as her chubby little hands reached up in the sunlight, trying to touch the crown. Her apple-like cheeks were framed by green willow leaves and blue, pink, and purple flowers. I listened to her giggle and to the whispered music of the willow trees and the water in the pond, a melody that had long been lost and forgotten, but now found its way back with a haunting spring fragrance.

Xianren? Yes, I heard some people call me that. How can that be? I am just a plain old man. Nothing xian about me.

Yes, I did jump out of that tower, about one story higher than the building, and survived. Look at me now. I didn't have a broken neck, shattered bones, paralyzed limbs, or worse, a permanently damaged brain that would turn me into a cabbage, a rotten one, at that.

No, I would rather be dead. But look at me. That was over thirty years ago. I was in my early thirties. Now I am in my seventies. Whatever I had back then is still with me now. All these parts are original, I tell you. I have heard that nowadays lots of folks my age have their knees or other joints replaced by plastic ones. Not me. Not me. I still have my own knees, my own bones. They are my best buddies. With that jump, from that height, any other bones would be crushed to pieces, but not mine, not mine.

What? Like a cat? Yeah, you heard that too. A cat can never break its bones no matter how high it falls. Its bones are elastic and supple, like they are made of liquid or something. It is no joke when people say that a cat has nine lives. It does not die easily. But I am not a cat. I am a human being. I have only one life. And I don't have those resilient limbs and bones. Yet when I jumped from that tower, my bones somehow didn't break and managed to maintain their shape.

They are still in good shape, you know. See the way I stretch my legs in this horizontal position? See the way I am standing upside down on my hands and how straight my legs are, just like this tree? See this line here? Whatever movements I make, advancing, retreating, turning around, or jumping, I can do it all on this line. The key is to keep the body in perfect balance, as stable as a mountain.

Yes, you are right. This is partly shaoling boxing. It stresses the strength, quickness, with steady rhythm. What, tai chi boxing? Oh yes, I like that too. Very different, though. Much slower. It has beautifully and smoothly strung movements like floating clouds and flowing streams. Shaoling, tai chi, or any other kind of martial art all stress a kind of circular, spiral type of movement. It is this movement that helps you keep the balance. Whatever you do, you must not lose it. This is the chi—the inner energy that sustains your body and retains its vitality.

How did I learn this? Well, to tell you the truth. I used to be a wusheng, *a martial hero, as it is called. I am sure you have watched the Beijing Opera before; you know what I am talking about. You must have seen those martial heroes who fly through the air back and forth on the stage? Their role is that of valiant warriors who risk their lives to fight for justice against evil forces with their superhuman martial feats. They do somersaults. They flip over, they jump up and down, and they can even freeze themselves in midair. Have you watched* the Journey to the West, *the fearless and matchless Monkey King? Well, that would be my role, a martial hero.*

Am I still acting? No, not any more. I left the stage ever since that jump. I have a new stage now. Right here around this tree, with these willow branches hanging overhead, green grass carpet spreading underneath my feet. And this spring air, this fresh April morning air. Oh, I tell you, it is like a fairyland, my fairyland.

Come, would you like to sit here under this tree for a while? It has been here for many years. Nobody knows its exact age. Some people say three hundred, others even longer. Look at this trunk. You and I cannot embrace it even if we hold our arms together. Look around you. Close your eyes. Smell the fragrance of these willow leaves. Feel the gentle touch of the spring breeze. Run your finger through this smooth and soft grass fresh with morning dew and listen to the water sing. You can't find a more quiet and beautiful place here in this city.

Do I come here every morning? Yes. Every day, for all these years. Suyi and I promised each other we would meet here at this willow tree every day in the spring, in April, our season; she practiced her voice and I my moves, just like we used to. We need to absorb the energy, chi, of the earth and then let this chi circulate freely through our bodies so that we can keep our balance.

Who is Suyi? She is an old friend. A sweet, dear old friend. Like my own sister. She is also my partner. On the stage, I mean. But she is a much brighter star. She is the female lead in our opera troupe, playing the role of both Hua Dan and Qingyi Dan, those brave, bright, and beautiful fairies. Whatever role she is playing on the stage, Suyi herself is like a fairy. If you watch the way she moves her high-soled shoes with such graceful gaits, the way she waves up and down her long white silk and satin stream sleeves, the way she swirls her bright colored skirt into a beautiful canopy, you would know what I mean. And her voice, oh, that is the voice of a fairy. Everyone from our opera troupe says so. I don't know what a fairy's voice sounds like, but when Suyi sings, that must be it.

Where is Suyi now? I will tell you where. Look up at this willow tree. She is here. What? You can't see her? She is right here beside me, somewhere around this tree. You may not see her, but I can. I come here every morning and talk to her. I know she is always waiting for me. Whenever I begin my exercises, she will practice her singing and dancing, exactly like we used to do. This was our favorite place to begin our daily practice and still is. Thirty years ago, every morning before sunrise, Suyi and I would come here to this tree and practice our routine for about an hour or so. Afterward, we would sit down against the tree trunk, with willow leaves swinging overhead, and watch the sun rise from behind the beautiful golden-orange horizon. Suyi loved to weave crowns of all sizes with willow branches and wild flowers. I learned it from her. She often wore one on her long and black velvet hair while she practiced dancing. Sometimes she let her hair cascade down onto her shoulders, and other times she had it loosely tied into a ponytail that swayed against her apple-green blouse. Often she would put one crown on my head and pull me over to dance with her. We would both keep spinning until we were too dizzy to stand, then we both fell onto the grass, out of breath, still laughing . . .

*O*h, *what did you say? Am I all right? I am fine. I am fine. Thank you. What? Suyi and me? No, no. Suyi was very shy about the men and women stuff. Once she is off the stage, she is timid almost like a little girl. She looked up to me as her older brother. We started training together when we were about eight years old. We both graduated from the school and then stayed here, teaching and performing in the school's opera troupe. So many years, we were used to being together; we never thought of anything else. I was content that I could see her and be with her every day. We were young then and thought we had plenty of time.*

Then came the summer of 1966 and ten chaotic years after that. Oh, those crazy days. Called upon by Chairman Mao and his Communist Party, people were mobilized to engage in the Great Proletarian Cultural Revolution intended to purge all enemies of the Party, wherever they might exist. Students were organized into Red Guards and others into various factions of Red Rebels. They took as their glorious mission to destroy the old world, embodied in the Four Olds—old ideology, old culture, old habits, old customs. Overnight, our troupe had become one of the central targets of this revolutionary storm. All the traditional operas we performed in the past years were now "poisonous weeds" that must be rooted out. Our directors were cast aside; all the costumes were burned and the backstage turned into a garbage site. Most of our exercise rooms on the top floor in the tower were converted into temporary jail cells. The theater itself was now a battlefield where every two or three days a major meeting would be held during which people from various groups fought with one another to show who were the most loyal revolutionaries.

No stage, no performance, no place for exercise, what could we do? Just step aside. With the curtain drawing up and down, you watched real-life drama unfolding every day. Today you saw this one slashing his wrist; tomorrow you heard that one hurling himself out of a window from a high building. It was like everybody started losing their minds at the same time, although I would say we didn't have our minds to begin with. We were so used to depending on the Party to think for us that our minds just got rusty and unable to function. Our energy was burned up, and chi drained out. Our bodies felt as light as air and as empty as balloons.

Suyi became a focused target now. All the plays she had performed became hard evidence against her. You know, those romantic love stories and fairy tales. Almost every major meeting we had in the theater was directed at her and several other leading figures of the troupe. By that time, the meetings were the only occasions when I could see her. My heart sank deeper each time I watched her standing in line on the stage, being yelled at and cursed, sometimes slapped and punched, by those Red Rebels. She looked at least ten years older now. Her body seemed to have shrunk underneath her dark blue long-sleeve shirt and pants. Her face was pale, screened in part by some of her shortened, dried strands of hair. Her head and shoulders leaned forward and her hands were folded at the chest as if she was trying to keep herself from falling onto the floor. No matter how long the meeting was and how loudly people were shouting, she never once raised her eyelids or uttered any sound. It was as if she were not there at all, having wandered away like a cloud, or a fairy.

One late night after one of these denunciation meetings, I was awakened by an urgent knocking. I opened the door. It was Suyi. She looked different now from the Suyi I saw at those meetings. Her hair was neatly fixed by two black butterfly hairpins on both sides. Her face was not as pale as before; it was obvious that she had applied some light makeup. Instead of that baggy dark blue shirt and pants, she was wearing a white silk and satin gown with its buttons tightened from her neck and winding down underneath her left arm in the shape of a half-moon.

She floated into the room, like a shadow, her eyes gleaming in the predawn darkness.

"Ming, I come here to say good-bye to you."

"What? Where are you going?" I didn't know she could go anywhere at this time.

"I will tell you when I get there."

Her whispery voice rippled through the darkness and her liquid eyes darted past me before I could catch any of their waves. In the dim light her white satin was glowing quietly like frosted snow reflecting the cold and bright moonlight.

"You take good care of yourself, all right? I will be back and look for you."

"Do they allow you to leave?" I asked, *still struggling to fully wake up.*

"I believe so." Her face lit up. *"I will see you soon. Under that old willow tree. All right? I will be waiting for you there."*

Then she grasped both my hands with which she covered her face. The silky and soft skin of her face chilled and burned me alternatively. Then she quickly withdrew her hands, turned around and in an instant, she was gone. Her satin gown danced through the darkness like a slash of lightening.

I don't remember how long before I finally fell back into a deep sleep. It seemed as if I had never fully woken up, not even when those rebels barged into my dorm shouting and screaming, and grabbed the collar of my shirt and pushed me to the floor.

"Get up, you sly cunning snake!"

I sat up, my hands pressing to the hard cold concrete floor to support myself. My eyes were still closed. My head was spinning at such a dazzling speed that I knew if I opened my eyes, I would lose my balance and fall on the hard cement.

"You must confess. What is the relationship between you and Lin Suyi?"

I really couldn't hear them, you know. All I could do was to sit still to keep myself from falling.

"Hey, we are talking to you, hear us? What's with you and Lin Suyi?"

"Are you deaf or what?" Someone dashed to my right side and hit my arm.

"Do you hear us or not? Lin Suyi committed suicide, don't you know? She hanged herself. Under that old willow tree. What a nerve that woman has! She picked that willow tree to show her defiance? How dare she! What a curse to the whole school! How determined she was to break away from our Great Leader and our Party!"

I opened my eyes slowly and painfully but saw only a resplendent whiteness, like the sun was shining through mist. I closed my eyes again. The whiteness persisted, as if there was no more night.

Then I heard someone screaming at my ears, "Do you want to go back to sleep? You are dreaming! Come with us right now! You must write a confession letter detailing your relationship with Lin Suyi and her suicide. You must prove that she was the one who chose to go against the Party and against this great revolution!"

I don't remember what happened next. All was a blur. But somehow and sometime around noon that day, I found myself in one of those small cells in the Tower, where our exercise rooms were now partitioned by temporary walls. The euphemism for these cells was "self-criticism room," but a harsher and truer term would be niupeng, a cowshed, a place of punishment for those who were found guilty of crimes against the current revolutionary movement. I didn't have any idea what kind of crime I had committed, but it didn't matter. Here I was in this small confined cell, stuck between a student desk and a chair like a caged animal.

On the student desk was a thin notebook, a sharp-pointed fountain pen, and a small bottle of red ink. I twisted open the lid of the bottle and saw about half of the red ink left. I put the pen into the bottle, let it absorb the ink for a while and then took it out. The red ink was dripping slowly onto the white paper, spreading like a pool of blood. Suddenly I felt nauseous and wanted to throw up, but my throat was blocked as if by a burning stone. I closed my eyes again, trying to fall asleep, when I heard two women in the next cell whispering; their lowered voices drifted into my ear over the dust in the air.

"Have you heard it?"

"What? Suyi? I know, she was gone. Just like that."

"It is better that way, you know. No blood. I can't stand blood. Like the principal, cutting his wrist like that. Oh dear, did you see that blood? All over his place and on the stairs. I live across the hall from him, you know."

"I know. But at least his body was left intact. Did you see the piano teacher who jumped from the fifth floor? Oyooo, he looked like crushed tofu, head to toe."

"That's true. Suyi always looked neat. She wouldn't have it any other way, I suppose. I heard she did it under that old willow tree."

"That's what I heard too. Ah, as I said, that way goes quick and clean. Do you know she didn't use any rope?"

"What do you mean?"

"You know, the rope. They said she used the sleeves of her white satin dress, you know?"

"You don't say. They are made of silk. Soft but strong."

"Yeah."

*T*he two women's whispery voices droned on, but I couldn't hear any more. Half asleep, half awake, I dragged my exhausted body toward the only place in the room through which I could see daylight, a small, rectangular window. As I tried to unhook its rusty hinges, the glass windowpane popped open on its own, which startled me, but also made me feel relieved. I looked downward: the concrete pathway lay under the burning sun; from its surface a bluish vapor rose, flickering like smoke.

I rubbed my eyes a little bit. The sun hurt. It fell directly toward my face. I could hardly see anything. Feeling giddy and nauseous, I wanted to lie down somewhere, anywhere, for a good rest. I couldn't even sit straight at that desk in the chair. Nor could I face that blood-stained paper and the pointed blood-dripping pen. I inched closer to the windowsills and looked out. The dazzling sunlight made everything down there a blur, a quiet and motionless white. A simple jump into that whiteness would end it all. Blood or no blood, an intact or broken body, how would I know? And what does it matter? I used to wonder, with all the ways leading to one's end, why some, like that piano teacher, a friend of mine, chose to jump from a height. Now I am here, realizing that at a moment like this, you are no longer concerned with the fear of falling down; rather you see the open space of the emptiness below, which tempts and lures you to fall, into whose embrace you fly like a bird, only downward.

I climbed onto the window, and squeezed into that rectangular hole, and without even looking down, I plunged into the air.

I started floating, as if on a soft cloud. My body was hoisted, it seemed, by something underneath me. As I was falling down through the open space, it suddenly occurred to me that I hadn't been able to practice my martial feats for a long, long time. I felt an exciting urgency to stretch my limbs and let them embrace the air. In an instance, I found myself back *on the stage, doing what I used to do—rolling over, jumping, leg-snapping, single and double flying kicks, and flipping over and over again.*

By the time I reached the ground, I found myself landing in a perfectly balanced position. Several teenage boys who were playing nearby saw me falling and started screaming and running toward me. Three or five adults appeared from nowhere, from all directions, and started gathering around me. They gasped at the boys' hysterical retelling of what had happened and stared at me warily as if I were some kind of animal or alien. I guess they were trying to figure out if I were a real person or a ghost or, even more, what I was made of—jumping out of the tower at the top of the sixth floor and still standing in this straight posture.

What happened later? Well, I was arrested, of course, and brought to a larger room later on. This time I did have a charge, because I didn't write that confession letter as I was ordered to. But you know what, for some reason, they quickly let me go. In fact, I was spared all further troubles. The word went around that I had a magic chi in my body; some even conjectured that I might be a reincarnation of a spirit. Wu Hua Ba Men (five flowers and eight doors), you heard everything. Who could explain the mystery of my falling from that height without being hurt? If I were a cat, it might be possible, but I'm not, you know. So who can explain it?

But I knew it was no magic. And it was not what I did either. It was Suyi. She saved me. I don't know how, but it was she and I knew it. She was somewhere with me while I was flying down through that burning air. I heard her whispering to me. I smelled the fragrance of her hair, and I even touched her white satin sleeves that were supporting me from underneath and kept me from losing balance.

You look puzzled. Don't. I know what I am talking about. I am not crazy. I don't believe what people say, that she is gone. I never saw her body afterward. I was told that she was cremated the day after she hanged herself. But later on when I went to the funeral home with one of her pictures, guess what they said? They had never seen anyone like her brought in around that time. That was the only funeral home in the city back then. I remember what she told me that night when she was leaving. Wait for me under our willow tree, she said. And I know she will come back to me. And that is the only place where we can meet. It is here. It is under this old willow tree.

Don't look at me like that. I mean it. Like I said earlier, I can see her and hear her like nobody else can. Every morning, we meet here before the sun rises. She still practices her singing and dancing, and I of course my martial arts. When we finish practicing, we sit down as in the old days under this old willow tree. We will listen to the birds chirping and twittering, watch the dragonflies darting here and there above the smiling waters in the pond, feel the cool touch of the sparkling dews on the blades of grass, and weave for each other crowns of willow branches and wildflowers in the morning sunlight. When we were young, we didn't have much time to appreciate all these simple and beautiful things. We have so much to catch up on, you know. And here we are, finally, together. In our own fairyland.

Well, look at me, going on and on. I hope I didn't bore you. It is such a beautiful day. The time when these willows begin turning green and flowers begin blooming. It makes you feel like talking, you know? It is very nice chatting with you. Look at the baby. She is awake. She is smiling at us. Oh, how good it is to smile like that.

What? Will I be here tomorrow? Every day, every day, my friend. As long as the tree is here, I will be here talking with Suyi.

It is time for us to leave now. You have a good day, you and your beautiful baby girl. It is such a beautiful spring morning; enjoy it.

I was drawn away from my reverie by the baby's giggling. She was still holding that willow crown, swaying it back and forth, up and down, her silver-bell-like voice ringing through the willow trees and over the grassland.

I looked around, and saw a shadow in white floating through the willow trees before it gradually merged with the glowing morning sunlight. Then I heard a whisper of wind, laughing softly as it came to join the golden reflection of sunlight upon the shining waters in the pond.

I bent toward my daughter, wrapped my arms around her and lifted her up.

Xianren is right. It is such a beautiful spring morning.

槐花 *8*

The Girl under the Red Flag

About ten miles west of Hefei, the provincial capital where I was born and grew up, there is a mountain called Dashu Hill. At the foot of Dashu Hill is the Revolutionary Martyrs' Cemetery where Communist heroes who died before 1949 during the anti-Japanese war and the three civil wars between the Communist and National parties are buried. A few miles further west of the cemetery, a gray concrete memorial hall was built in the early 1980s in honor of those younger martyrs who sacrificed themselves during the revolutionary era in the 1960s and '70s.

As Communist Young Pioneers, we used to come to the Revolutionary Martyrs' Cemetery every April 5th for the Clear and Bright Festival—Tomb Sweeping Day—to pay tribute to our revolutionary predecessors, pledging our faith in Communism and our determination to continue its cause. Carrying on our backs bundled rolls like soldiers in a military drill and lining up in two rows, with our teacher in front holding a red flag, we would leave school before dawn and walk for about three hours from the east end, crossing the center part of the city, toward the west. It was always a sunny day, despite the fact that it was the beginning of a rainy season. By the time we arrived at the cemetery, it was almost around noon. Exhausted and starving, we had to go straight to the cemetery to start the tomb-sweeping and listen to war veterans' lectures about our responsibility as the young generation. After the lectures were over, we then hurriedly unpacked our lunches, gobbled them down, and then got ready for the best part of this trip—hiking.

Like a throng of wild birds caged for the entire day and now finally free to fly, we plunged into a flood of warm spring sunlight, releasing our energy in a high-speed race toward the top of the mountain, running through the groves and bushes, screaming at the top of our lungs, and chasing each other with all our might. A girl dressed in a white long-sleeve shirt and sky-blue pants was holding a red flag with both hands while running toward the mountaintop. We all followed her, thirty boys and girls, like soldiers in the battle-field aiming to take over the highest post while shouting, "Charge! Charge! See who gets to the top first!" Her voice was the loudest, ringing with energy and excitement, just as she was the fastest, far ahead of the rest of us, including the boys. She was always the first to arrive at our destination—the top of the mountain. Once there, she would wave the red flag back and forth while beginning to sing and dance, her two shoulder-length light brown braids bouncing to and fro, up and down, her clear and melodious voice resonating through the deep green bushes and her face beaming in the bright golden sun.

That was more than thirty years ago. You, that little girl with the red flag, are now resting in a dim and quiet corner inside the hall of the newly built memorial. Your sunshine smile is now frozen in a black-and-white photo frame hung on the stark and cold wall, a barren saline land where nothing could ever grow.

But once a year on the Clear and Bright Festival, I would go and visit you there in the memorial. I would be standing alone in that chilly and dimly lit hall, waiting for your frozen smile to melt, for you to come down from the wall, joining me in our annual spring reunion. Once our hands touched each other's, our bodies would become as light as feathers; together we would fly out of that cold and caged space into the warm and open grassland outside. There, basking in the bright spring sunshine, we twirled and swirled, our hands reaching out to the sparkling beads cascading through the brilliant sunlight. We tried to catch as many as we could, but they quickly fell through our fingers into the grass where they lay quietly, glistening hauntingly under the sun. We bent over, looking for them in the grass when our heads bumped into each other. We tried to laugh the pain away, but no sound came out from either of us. Then, when I straightened up my back, and turned around, you were gone. All I could see was your hand waving as your shadow receded toward the concrete memorial. For all this sunlight, this spring breeze, this green grass, and blue sky, I wasn't able to hold you a moment longer. I only hoped that we would be with each other again, on another sunny spring day soon.

We had been with each other since we were six and seven and were never apart until we were sixteen and seventeen. Together we grew up through ten seasons from Young Pioneers with red triangle scarves fluttering around our necks to members of the Communist Youth League with sickle and ax badges pinned to the left side of our chests. Remember at the eighth grade (the second year of our middle school) when our school, like everywhere else, was reorganized into different units modeled after military patterns—groups as squads, classes as battalions, grades as companies, and schools as regiments? That was the time we started working as close partners as well as best friends. For each class—battalion—there were two committees, the Youth League and the Study Committee. You, who had been our class monitor since the fourth grade, became chair of the Youth League and I, chair of the Study Committee. We had different responsibilities—yours was to oversee students' applications for membership in the Youth League and to organize various extracurricular activities; mine was to provide aid to teachers of all subjects, distributing and collecting study materials, helping students with poor grades, and most of all, editing our bulletin board. It was the golden rule at the time that political awareness must take precedence over everything else. But unlike the Youth League chairpersons from other battalions who felt superior and condescending to the Study Committee, you always showed enthusiasm and passion for everything that involved the Study Committee. Whenever you were available, you would help me design each issue of our bulletin board, drawing pictures, printing in calligraphy characters, and contributing articles when they were needed. Every Wednesday and Saturday we stayed late after school, working together, writing and drawing while chatting until sunset and dusk fell.

At age sixteen, we had so much to talk about and to look forward to. We couldn't wait to chase the dreams we cherished dearly. I knew you wanted to become a pilot. Your face glowed with excitement whenever you told me how much you wanted to fly across the blue sky like a soaring eagle, the bravest raptor. You showed me various clippings you had collected about flying: airplanes and pictures of the first generation of Chinese woman pilots. You were very serious about your dream, which was the reason you took part in team sports—basketball, volleyball, badminton, and gymnastics. All this physical training, you said, would not only strengthen your muscles, but also increase your physical stamina and mental capacity for stress.

My dream was to become an author, a famous one like my father, who had touched so many lives with his imaginative power. I loved reading novels and poems as much as you enjoyed studying the structure of an airplane. But our dreams had to become subordinate to a higher call—a call we pledged to live and die for when we raised our right arms in front of the red flag, first as Young Pioneers and later as Youth League members. Like our parents' generation, we were expected to take part in the glorious journey toward building a perfect Communist world. In a journey like this, there was simply no space for nor need to nurture any personal dreams because the noble mission dictated every move of each individual. No matter how high our dreams could fly, they would all eventually fall down onto the earth, both literally and metaphorically.

By the time we were about to graduate from high school in the spring of 1976, college entrance exams had been canceled for ten years. And there was neither sign nor hope for them to be reinstated. Millions of high school graduates, categorized by Chairman Mao as petty bourgeois intellectuals, many of them former Red Guards, had been dispatched since 1968 by Mao to the countryside and remote frontier areas to be reeducated by the poor and lower-middle-class peasants. It was what Mao called a much-needed thought reform through labor so that the young generation would not deviate from the red path laid down by the Great Leader. It was Chairman Mao's belief that educated people were inferior to illiterate peasant, and thus ought to emulate them. As he once put it, "Peasants have dirty hands and cowshit-sodden feet, but they are much cleaner than intellectuals."

Like those early graduates, the majority of us were to leave the city and settle down in the countryside for an indefinite period. All had to join this journey except those who happened to be an only child or to have high-ranking officials as parents. During a time when mothers were encouraged to model themselves on heroic Russian mothers who gave birth to as many children as they could, one child was a rare species. And those who could somehow get round by either joining the army or simply staying at home because of their parents' interference were merely a handful. Out of sixty classmates, fewer than five would be able to stay. You and I were among the majority since we both had an older sister working in the city.

So the question was not whether to go or not but rather where. After years and years of being taught to get ready to serve the Party's cause with heart and soul, we now realized the time had come when we should materialize the pledge we had made since we were six. We didn't exactly know or understand what we, sixteen-and seventeen-year-old-high school graduates, could be expected to do in the countryside, but we were young and full of enthusiasm and energy. We felt like eagles flying across a vast field under a clear blue sky to help our peasant teachers fight for a better future.

Months before graduation, I had consulted with my parents about possible destinations for this journey. Secretly, I had already set my mind to a place my father was very familiar with—the heart of the Dabei mountain area where my family had once lived for a year. Having read many war memoirs about those heroic battles fought on that land and, most of all, about peasants who were still struggling to stay alive, I thought it would be an ideal place for me to dedicate myself to its future. My father, however, had some reservations. He was visibly upset when I told him about my plan. After a long pause, he shook his head and said, "If you go there, in the winter you would be trapped by the mountain snow and couldn't get out till spring. Have you thought about that?"

Although being entrapped by the snow sounded to me like a remote possibility, it did make me realize how worried and concerned my parents were for their teenage daughter to go alone to some far-off mountainous area. To alleviate their concerns, I eventually agreed to go to my father's home village in Chaohu County, about two hundreds miles away from Hefei. It was, I could see, a small relief for them to know that I would be among kin, most of whom carried the same last name, Lu.

You, on the other hand, decided to join one of those military camp organizations called Jianshe Bintuan—a large collective farm where young graduates were organized, as in schools, into military units (squad, battalion, company, and regiment). They lived in dorms and had to adhere to very restrictive rules and work on their own farmland. At the very beginning, you told me that you would go to one of those farms and tried to persuade me to go with you. "It would be such an open land. Think about it, Jiang. Think about how much we can do to help build a brand new type of farmland!" Your voice resonated with excitement and hope, just as it did when you talked about your dreams of becoming a pilot. I admired your courage for making that brave choice, feeling a little ashamed of my taking shelter in my father's home village, the image of which was far less glorious and promising. The only comfort was that it would at least give my parents some peace of mind—more or less.

So, for the first time since we had known each other, we would soon part. Before our departure, there would be a farewell ceremony at the city hall plaza by the Hefei City Revolution Committee. All the graduates from fifty middle and high schools in Hefei—several thousand of them—would gather for the last time before embarking on their journeys. But we wouldn't be able to stay with our fellow graduates from the same school. Once our destinations had been determined, all the classes were then disbanded, and we were designated to the work units of our parents, a more efficient way to keep track of and control our whereabouts. If any of us didn't go as planned, our parents would be held responsible and subsequently punished. Neither you nor I worried, however, that we wouldn't be together at the meeting. We knew each other's parents' work units— yours in the Bureau of Transportation and mine in Culture and Entertainment—and thought we would find each other easily.

Before the meeting, I reported to and registered with the Bureau of Culture and Entertainment to which both my parents' work units belonged and was given a small rectangular certificate card with a red plastic cover on which were written three golden letters: *Guang Rong Zheng*, meaning: Honor Card. Inside there were two pages. On the left side were my name, picture, birthday, and birthplace, and on the right my parents' names, their resident address, work unit, and the place I was about to settle in. We were to pin these cards on our chests during the ceremony and then keep them as our certificates for being part of this grand journey.

About a week before this scheduled meeting, on a beautiful early spring afternoon, we ran into each other near the school entrance; you were coming out and I was going in. We both were in a hurry, but we did manage to chat for a little while. We showed each other our honor cards and compared them, joking about our photos but feeling a little sad over the two different destinations: yours Feidong, mine Chaohu. "Cheer up," you comforted me. "We will write, at least once a week. We will visit each other. I will see you again at the meeting, remember?" You flashed that familiar sunshine smile at me then turned and started running. As you crossed the street and vanished in a sea of people, your voice darted back and echoed at my ears: "See you there! See you at the meeting!"

But we never got to see each other, then or ever again.

The meeting was to be held in early March, my birth month. When the day came, the spring seemed suddenly to turn its back on us. It was cold and windy. The sullen sky sagged lower and started drizzling early in the morning. Around ten o'clock when I got to the plaza joining the thousands of other graduates, a cold, hard rain started pouring, a heavy, silencing kind of rain which fell soundlessly into a forest of red flags and banners fluttering over the huge dark-headed crowed and blotting the sky above. As far as eyes could see, the whole plaza was like a surging ocean of red waves gleaming with rainwater.

It was so easy to be lost in that vast ocean. Neither you nor I found each other.

The first few weeks in my home village were disappointing and depressing. I wasn't prepared for what I saw: backward farming, tough and tedious fieldwork from rice planting and harvesting to weeding and cotton-picking. It was nothing like what I had imagined or seen in documentary films in which peasants, men and women, old and young, were always in high spirits, riding a tractor or a combine, crossing neatly plowed square or rectangular fields, their arms waving with excitement and faces beaming with enthusiasm. In my village, small, shapeless rice paddies lay languidly, scattered here and there like discarded pieces of cloth in a deserted tailor's workshop. There were no tractors, only old cattle pulling plows with unsteady and fragile legs, their downcast eyes darkened with shyness and modesty. The villagers, laboring in the field all day long, looked worn out and exhausted. Most of them were my kin and treated me as if I were a distinguished though unneeded guest who was just paying a short visit to my old home on behalf of my father, who was held in high respect among the villagers. It didn't take long for me to realize that there were no heroic battles for me to fight here, no sacred pledge to fulfill, and no mission to accomplish. The glorious dream turned into an empty hole I hardly knew how to fill.

But you were as enthusiastic and exuberant as ever. We wrote to each other frequently, almost every week. Each letter was at least two or three pages long. While mine were burdened with bitter complaints and despondency, yours brimmed with excitement and expectations. In each of your letters, you tried to cheer me up, encouraging me to think far ahead and to make more effort to learn valuable things from peasants. In fact, you said you envied me for being among peasants, since there were very few in your farm corps. Nevertheless, you were still excited about each day, about what you had done so far—plowing the land, planting seeds, and harvesting crops in the field. In almost all these letters, you discussed the possibility of zhageng—"taking root," a popular term for permanently settling down in the countryside. Every now and then, you would still talk about your dream of becoming a pilot, but you stressed that if the Party needed us young generation to stay in the countryside, then you would do it without any regret.

Your enthusiasm and faith rekindled my confidence about the future. The first step was, I decided, to truly become one with the peasants and reform myself through hard labor. Instead of living with my grandparents as my parents would have hoped, I chose to move into a small mud-brick and thatched house which I shared with two other students. I also declined a proposal from the head of the village that I work as a bookkeeper in the mill for the production team and decided to join the women and girls' teams for fieldwork. Soon summer came, the time the villagers called double-sizing season, which usually lasted about a month. It was an intensified period of labor during which the early season rice must be harvested and the late season rice be planted simultaneously. Both needed to be finished by the end of July. Like most of the villagers, I got up at about five in the morning and went to the rice paddy, pulling out rice shoots until dawn. Then I went home for a brief breakfast and returned to the field again to plant rice until noon. Then two hours after lunch, we would go and cut rice under the scorching July sun until after dusk.

Every morning when I was awakened by our production team leader's shrill whistle coupled with his husky yet energizing voice: "Elderly go to the peanut field. Women and girls all go to the rice patch in the east . . ." I struggled to get up, half awake and half asleep, one foot lower and one foot higher, stepping out like a drunk or a sleepwalker into the thick predawn darkness. I tried to convince myself that this was part of a grand march and a glorious mission, and that I was doing something worthwhile. As each day got hotter and hotter and the fieldwork more and more intense, I soon found no energy to think about the journey or the mission any more. The monotonous and backbreaking labor of pulling, planting, and harvesting rice numbed my body and emptied my mind. My eyes ached and my head swelled with shooting headaches; often I walked in the field as if treading the clouds. From predawn to dusk, I moved in and out, like a robot. A bitter emptiness encroached on me and clutched my throat so tightly that I could hardly breathe. Then on one of those blazing July days, I wished I had stopped breathing altogether.

It was approaching noon. We had been bending over under the burning sun since early morning, cutting rice in a rice paddy about a mile east of the village. As I stood up and stretched myself, I saw the mailman in his light green uniform riding a bicycle fast in our direction. Its old and rusty wheels squeaked as it rolled nearer and nearer. It was odd to see him on that day, since he delivered mail only every other day and had come yesterday.

"Telegram! Telegram!"

All of the women and girls working in the field stopped. We all looked at each other in dread. During those days, a telegram was always the bearer of bad news. People hadn't got used to the idea of using the medium to send good news—there wasn't much anyway. Everyone seemed to hold their breath and hope that the telegram and whatever trouble it could bring were for someone else.

In an instant of distraction, my sickle slipped and cut my left middle finger. The blood dripped into the dark brown water, undulating small red ripples that trembled away. To stop the bleeding, I pressed my right thumb on the cut and then quickly put the finger into the muddy water. The initial pain pierced through me like a sharp needle. My head was spinning. I closed my eyes for a while and then took it out. The cut, in the shape of a small sickle, was now swollen and pale. It felt numb, and so did I.

Then I heard my name called.

"Telegram! For you, Sanzi!"

All eyes turned toward me and fixed me where I was. I tried to pull my legs out of the mud, but my feet were stuck and couldn't get out. The mailman handed the telegram to the woman closest to the edge of the rice paddy and it was passed in silence from hand to hand until it finally reached me on the other side of the field.

I took the telegram. It was a small piece of paper, half of a letter size, with light green square boxes filled by black characters. I saw your name, in pitch black ink, side by side with four other characters, framed by green-lines:

Wei Zhong Xi Sheng Su Gui. "Weizhong sacrificed. Return home soon."

The sender was my mother.

The piece of paper fell through my fingers onto the surface of the dark water, floating in circles. I heard whispers and murmurs rising from behind me like a faint heat wave that was gradually sweeping me away. But I held my foot firm in the mud and waited, waited for you to break free from those green boxes and talk to me one more time.

Where are you now? What does this mean? Didn't you just send me that letter and a picture in which you are driving a tractor, waving to me with that sunshine smile? Didn't we promise each other we would visit? Are you still there waiting for me?

I dropped my sickle in the mud, bundled up the last bunch of rice I had just cut, and placed it down beside me. The golden grain lay quietly under the sun, waiting to be carried away, threshed, and shelled.

With everything still a blur, I trudged my way for ten miles to the nearest bus station, and by about three in the afternoon, I barely caught the last bus to the city. As usual, the bus was packed with peasants and students like me. I was sandwiched in like a sardine, my feet dangling helplessly in the air. All the way my mind sank into a coma from which I didn't want to awake.

The bus pulled up at the terminal located two blocks away from your home in the Provincial Bureau of Transportation. It was about seven o'clock when I entered the complex where your parents lived. We used to come to your home at least twice a week. Whenever we did, we would be greeted by a friendly old man who came out of the reception room, chatting with us, sometimes giving us candy or other goodies. But he wasn't here today and the door was closed. I slowed my steps as I approached the third row of the red-brick houses. Yours would be the one at the end. As soon as I saw the brown double doors—which looked so painfully familiar—I wanted to stop and turn back. I didn't know if you would be there or not. I dreaded taking one more step. But it was too late. I already heard someone sobbing. There was a small group of people gathering in the living room; one of the girls with red puffy eyes came up to greet me and ushered me to your mother's bedroom. Aunt Kang lay against the headboard, both her hands covering her face. As soon as I walked in, she turned toward me, reached out her hands, and burst into a heart-wrenching wail:

"Oh, Shujiang, Shujiang! Weizhong is gone! Weizhong is gone! She is still a baby! She is not eighteen yet! Oh heaven, tell me, tell me, how can this be real? How can this be happening?!"

Oh, how hurtful it was to see your mother in such distress— your mother who I remembered as having only the brightest smile to shine upon us and the funniest stories to make us laugh. I knelt down at the edge of her bed, holding her cold, wet hands, buried my head in them and started crying for the first time since I received the telegram. My body was shaking so violently that it seemed to be falling apart and I couldn't even bother to pick up the pieces.

You died, your mother told me, as a hero. You gave your own life to save two other seventeen-year-old girls in a pond near the farm. When these two girls were trapped in the deep part of the pond and screamed for help, you were the first to rush into the water to pull one of them to the bank. I knew that among all sports, you liked swimming the least. You once joked that you would be an eagle staying far away from water. Remember that last summer before graduation? We promised ourselves that we must learn how to swim. Four of us, including our other two good friends, went to the city swimming pool every day, but unfortunately, none of us made any real progress since we spent more time chatting and playing in the water rather than swimming. But you must have put all that aside, thinking only how to rescue your comrades. When you went back trying to save the other one, you were so exhausted that without a sound you slipped into the deep bottom of the pond. By the time people pulled you out, your lungs had been choked with so much water that you couldn't breathe any more. But both girls were fine and were right beside your mother's bed, crying.

I told them not to cry. You would like to see them happy, just as you always wanted me to be. Only I am still waiting, waiting for you to come back to me. I want to be happy—together with you.

I kept my eyes wide open on my way back to the bus stop across the street. This was the stop where we had met and bid many good-byes. You would always stand beside the cement lamppost, waiting for me, smiling and waving long before or after the bus pulled up and took off. The dusty orange bus rumbled near in the gathering dusk. I mustered all the energy I had left and barely squeezed myself into the crowded bus. I raised my right arm and waved toward the empty bus stop, imagining what you would look like standing there, if alive, after these six months on the farm. I never got to see you; your body was cremated the day before I received my telegram because of the extremely warm weather. I don't know if I would have wanted to see you that way even if I could. Whoever was lying there, would not have been you. You are here, with me, that little girl holding a red flag, singing and dancing on the mountaintop, your face radiating smiles and strength under the warm and beautiful spring sunshine.

This image of you sustained me all the way through my journey back to my parents'. By the time I got home, it was past supper time; the dishes and bowls had been put on a small round folding table. My grandma was sitting beside the table, waiting for me. My parents, who were both home at the time, hurried out from their bedroom and greeted me with wordless smiles. I returned their concerned eyes with silence; my throat constricted, unable to bring out any words. My mind seemed to have lost the function of responding or reacting to outside signals, including my grandma's gentle reminder to have my supper.

I put down my travel bag on one of the wooden chairs and looked around for the familiar family dinner table, the heavy wood square one with eight immortals carved around its four legs. It had been moved into my parents' bedroom where it would serve as an emergency shelter for the entire family in case of an imminent earthquake, which as predicted by both national and local weather stations, could occur anytime now. In both urban and rural areas, every household was ordered to prepare some kind of shelter for itself. No one in this region had ever experienced an earthquake, but all knew it must be the most dreadful and deadly natural disaster. Nobody could easily escape when it did happen: you could survive a fire, flood, or hurricane maybe, but how could you possibly escape from the earth itself? When it cracked and dragged you down, there would be no way out for anyone.

I went into my parents' bedroom and approached our shelter. For our one-story apartment, this big square table would presumably shield my family from the falling roof. I crouched into this shelter and sat down on a big bamboo mat spread underneath the table. I couldn't stretch my back and sit straight, or my head would bump into the hard wood bottom of the table. Those four solid wooden legs surrounded me, on which the carved figures of immortals and fairies were dancing a silent dance. Then I felt something trickling down my cheek. Water. Coming from my eyes. I tried to wipe it away, yet it only blurred my vision. Then you appeared. You looked tired, as if just returning from a long trip, your face a little swollen and eyes bleary, your hair loose on your shoulders, dripping with water, and you walked as if still in a yet fully waking dream.

"I miss you," you whispered, your eyes gazing into mine.

"Me too. How long can you stay?"

"I don't know. I don't have any sense of time anymore."

"Will you be back?"

"I think so."

"Promise?"

"Promise."

You then smiled at me, and I smiled back.

That was all what we had; that was all we needed.

The earth may quake; the river may go dry, but that smile stays.

Now you are resting in that gray concrete memorial, and your seventeen years of life are frozen into that black-and-white photo. Both the memorial and the cemetery next to it have become desolate and forgotten. Weeds have overgrown the crevices of the tombstones and the inside of the memorial hall is as empty as it is creepy. Nobody comes here anymore. In the mid-1980s, the Metropolitan Landscaping Committee built a public park on the other side of the hill. People gathered with their families for spring outings and summer picnics, adults sitting on the green grass in the sunlight chatting and playing poker, children chasing each other in their games of hide-and-seek. No one would bother to come to this side, either to the cemetery or to the memorial. These are places haunted by silent spirits and ghosts that belonged to a past people want to forget, a past burdened with too much pain and perplexities.

But it doesn't matter. Whether we choose to remember or to forget, those ghosts will always be among us, and we among them. It is where the stories and lives began. To continue our journey in this world we need to listen to these stories and to learn the beginning of everything: what happened, why it happened, what should have or not have been, what could have been and what still might be. In remembering the past, we have chosen to confront it, to pick up its pieces and to find what we've lost. We know that the wounds will open but we also know that they will heal. So here I am, every spring, on April 5th, the Tomb Sweeping Day, coming to see you and be with you. In the season swelled with hope and dreams, we are together on the green hills, on the grassland, and under the spring sun. Holding each other's hands, we sing, dance, and laugh, our arms reaching high into the blue sky, like the wings of two eagles.

The last time we were with each other in the memorial hall was the spring of 1991, two years after the 1989 bloodshed in Tiananmen Square that stunned me into a depressing silence and eventually prompted my decision to leave the country. But I have not left you. We may have lost each other in that surging ocean of red flags, but our dreams have once again found us together, taking us once more to the top of the mountain where I watch you dance and listen to you sing under the red flag in the bright spring sunlight.

槐花 *9*

A World of Rain

When my mother, an art student, married my father, a young
novelist and playwright, on a rainy Saturday in the spring of 1953,
she could have dressed in a traditional Chinese wedding gown—qi
pao—embroidered in fine red silk thread with the traditional wedding symbols of phoenix and peony. She could have had her thick
brown hair permed, curled, or rolled into the full moon of a bun, or
she could have simply let it cascade down onto her shoulders. She
could have put on some jewels, like the freshwater pearl necklace, a
wedding gift from her mother, or the diamond-shaped dark blue
brooch with a white orchid engraved inside, an engagement present
from her fiancé, my father. She could have danced all night with her
groom to romantic music, or she could have sung one of those
church songs she'd learned when she was a member of a Catholic
school choir.

She may have thought about all those possibilities but only with
a very keen awareness that she couldn't do any of them, for the simple
reason that they were not quite appropriate for a revolutionary style
wedding ceremony as expected for her and her groom. So on that
warm rainy spring day, one of many regular working Saturday
evenings, my mother, after returning from class, went back to her
dorm room that she shared with three other girls, picked up her
green canvas suitcase prepacked with all her clothing and other

127

belongings, bid good-bye to her friends, and hurried into the drizzling rain toward a new and unknown journey. As usual, she wore her gray blue double breasted jacket called Lenin jacket, a popular suit for working women at the time, the counterpart of a man's Mao uniform, light brown khaki trousers, and homemade black cloth shoes. She braided her hair into two long plaits, only this evening she tied two blue satin ribbons at the end of each plait. She didn't wear any jewelry, nor did she expect to have any music for the wedding.

In fact, she felt as if she were just going to one of the many political meetings or to one of her classes; only she knew that he would be there waiting for her, the man whose life would merge with hers from tonight onward. The small hotel room rented for them by her fiancé's work unit—the Provincial Association of Literature and Art—would be their temporary home. In the room there were two chairs, a wooden square table, two small stools, and a double wooden bed, all bearing the red stamps of my father's work unit. The double bed, which was actually two single ones pushed together, was covered with a blue and white striped bed sheet. At the headboard lay a pair of pillows and at its end a folded roll, all with similar blue and white strips. In one corner of the room, standing side-by-side against the wall, were two large canvas suitcases, one dark brown belonging to my father, and the other light green, my mother's, leaning on each other, waiting for a life together, like their respective owners.

The guests had already gathered around the table on which sat four large glass bowls. Two of them were mounds of hard and soft wedding candies in colorful wrappers; in the other two were packets of wedding cigarettes—Flying Horse with a white winged horse flying across the blue sky and Crossing Yangtze River with several sailing boats full of the People's Liberation Army soldiers crossing the Yangtze River in the final battles that eventually forced the National Party to retreat to Taiwan. Women guests chewed candies while the men smoked. Two officials from my father's work unit were there to preside over the wedding. My mother's feeling that she was attending another political meeting was not totally unfounded. The two officials started the ceremony by giving a short speech in which they encouraged the newly wedded couple to work hard to contribute to the new future of the country. Next the bride and groom were asked to say something about how they met each other and about their future plans. The ceremony then ended in a blur of chatting, candies being eaten and cigarettes puffing.

As the evening deepened, the guests started leaving. They shook hands in turn with the bride and groom, now husband and wife, congratulating them one more time before disappearing into the rain and darkness. After seeing off the last guest and cleaning away all the candy wrappers and cigarette butts, my mother and father sat down on the bed, their arms around each other, listening to the soft and steady rhythm of the falling rain, waiting for a beautiful and clear-blue sky tomorrow.

I was 21 when I married your father, the year I was graduating from the provincial art school. I was born under the sign of the Rooster, a more common word for a phoenix. Did I tell you that I had a twin sister? When we were born, my grandma was very disappointed since my father was the only son in Zhang family. But after my sister died suddenly in her sleep when we were about ten months old, I became more precious in the eyes of my grandma. She said I was living a double life, that of my sister as well as my own. She asked a fortune-teller to read my palm, and afterward she claimed that I was a phoenix born under a lucky star and should be allowed to do whatever I chose to do, including going to school so that I could have a bright future—although she and I might have different interpretations of the word "future."

In the old days, girls were brought up to believe that the best life for them was to marry a decent husband and have children—especially boys—so that the family name could be passed on. For most girls, it was not a chosen destiny, but a route they were expected to take, like my mother and grandma had. But I wanted to travel a different road, to pursue different dreams, dreams that sounded crazy back then—to be an artist or an opera singer. With my father's flour mill developing steadily, he could afford to send me to a local private Catholic school run by foreign missionaries. That was the first time I took art and music classes. I also joined the church choir. All the nuns, we called them momos, told me what a beautiful voice I had. One of them volunteered to give me voice lessons. I spent much of my free time there, learning English, painting, singing, and helping around with whatever chores needed to be done.

But at home, my mother and grandmother had already started planning my future. When I was about fifteen, my mother and grandmothers began seriously engaging themselves in finding me a suitable family to marry into. A stout matchmaker frequently paid visits to our house. She showed my grandmother and mother cards and notes on which were written the birthdays and horoscopes of boys; she compared them with mine to make sure that there was no ill match and that a marriage would be harmonious. By that time, the war between the Communist and National Parties had intensified, and the Communists led by Mao were winning. The Catholic school was closed and the momos were forced to leave the country. I stayed at home most of the time, resigning myself to the fate of a "lucky" girl, i.e., to become an obedient wife and a virtuous mother like my mother and grandmothers before me.

When Mao and his Communist Party won the war in 1949, I was almost sixteen. Like many of my fellow countrymen and women, I was overjoyed, having learned from propaganda that the Red Army was an army for the people and that the Communist Party's highest goal was to build up a harmonious society in which everyone would be given equal opportunities—men and women alike. Women and girls were told that they were the "females of a new era" who could and should hold up half the sky along with the men. Just imagine! Holding up half the sky! Despite my mother's and grandmother's objections—they thought studying art was a crazy idea for a girl—I took an entrance exam for the provincial art school and left home for Hefei, the capital city of the province. I no longer had to worry about being married off to some stranger and living my life dutifully as a wife and a mother. I could pursue my dream of becoming an artist and a singer, a dream that seemed to be shining over me like a beautiful morning sun.

And in that beautiful sunshine came your father. He was tall and handsome, kind and charming, an author of several novels and short story collections. He was also the editor in chief for our provincial literary magazine. That was how we first got to know each other—through correspondence when I submitted poems to that magazine. We finally met in person when he came to our school to give lectures. In the following months he often visited my dorm. At first, we—he, four other girls, and I—would get together and chat. Then one day he invited me to go out with him alone. He knew there was a birch forest near the campus. It was a sunny spring day. So off we went.

That first time and many times afterward we would go sit at the edge of a clear-water creek that wound through the forest, listening to the birds singing and watching the sun go down behind the trees. There were wildflowers around us—yellow, blue, pink, purple, and white. Your father often picked one or two and put them in my hair. He would hold my hands in his, and tell me the stories he was working on and those he was thinking about, or read to me what he had just written. Sometimes I brought my sketch pad and painting board, drawing everything that surrounded us: the birches with their thoughtful eyes, the creek with its rapid current, the wildflowers with their robust colors, the sun with its purple and golden-red twilight.

During that spring, we went there almost every evening, even in the rain. I remember one of those rainy evenings. We stood beside the creek, now swollen with rainwater, your father holding a big yellow oilcloth umbrella over us. We listened to the raindrops falling through the leaves and to the creek laughing in its rushing waters. We stood there, our arms around each other, holding onto our umbrella in a world of rain, waiting for those raindrops lying colorless on the grass to turn into a rainbow in our lighted hearts. Those were the moments when I realized for the first time that I had a piece of sky I could call my own, the moments when I thought and believed that all the dreams we dreamed together and all the promises we made to ourselves and to each other would come true.

What she didn't know at the time was that the rain would not stop. In a few years, it would turn into a horrendous flood that washed away everything that she once owned—those moments, those dreams, the promises she and my father had made to themselves and to each other.

It didn't take long for mother to realize that whatever dream she had for herself, she must fold it over and hide it in the deep pocket of her heart, not allowing it to see the light again. Under the leadership of Chairman Mao and his Party, a new society had to be tailored and a new people needed to be created. In the spring of 1963, while the nation was still struggling to survive the worst famine in modern times, the Great Leader called on people to learn from a perfect model, an ordinary soldier named Lei Feng. Growing up as an orphan, Lei Feng regarded himself to be the Party's son, whose highest life goal was to follow the Party and its great leader Chairman Mao and to dedicate himself whole-heartedly to the Party's cause. His good deeds and self-sacrifice were told in *Lei Feng Diary*, to be read and studied by everyone in the nation. Lei Feng was willing to be a bright, shiny cog in the machinery of the revolution and every citizen must model themselves on him and do the same.

Like millions of other fellow citizens, mother strove to be one such well-functioning cog in the revolutionary machine. The lives of these human cogs were defined and measured only by the depth of their faith in and the degree of their devotion to the Party. To survive was to live out this definition and be up to its measurement. There were no other alternatives: people learned from experiencing and witnessing one political movement after another that any sign of deviation—seen by the Party as disobedience—would lead only to self-destruction. To live meant to abstain from one's own desire and to abandon one's dreams.

So my mother, like many others in her generation, obediently and unconditionally accepted any tasks or assignment requested of her by the Party. This loyal dedication started when she first obeyed the order to work as a librarian in the Anhui provincial library shortly after she married. Jobs, like everything else, were assigned to individuals by various levels of Party committees. Mother, of course, swallowed her bitter disappointment and resigned herself to this first assignment that would be followed by many others. Starting in 1953, the year she married my father, and continuing throughout the 1970s, my mother's life was a swirling top—a top spun by an invisible hand as endless political storms ravaged the land, one after the other: land reform, the Four Clean-ups, the Anti-Rightist campaign, the Big Leap Forward, and then the Cultural Revolution. For her, the burden was all the heavier because she became a mother of four children, whom she was forced to leave behind whenever she was called to duty.

As each day went by, her dream of becoming an artist or singer drifted farther and farther away from her. Exhaustion had seeped into her bones and was written on her face; it showed in her every move. Two months after my oldest sister was born in the spring of 1954, my mother had to go to a rural area about two hundred miles away from the city and her child. The calls to duty continued after she gave birth to three more children, and never seemed to end. Lacking both time and energy to take care of her four young children, my mother got help from her mother, my grandma, who traveled back and forth between her own home in Bangbu and Hefei where we lived. When my grandma had to return to my grandfather's, the four of us would be sent to a boarding day-care center and come home only once a week. Whenever my mother recalled how, on each Saturday evening, we four small children would stand close to each other, crowded with other kids, craning our necks, our little hands holding on tightly to the iron bars of the gate of the day-care center as we waited for our mother or father to pick us up, she would burst into tears, her voice trembling, "You all looked like poor little miserable prisoners behind those iron bars."

I wanted to cry each time I saw you waiting for me at the other side of that gate. I wanted to stay home to take care of you, just like my own mother took care of me and my brothers. I missed the first day you began rolling over, the first time you started walking, your first tooth, and your first word. I wanted to stay home longer and didn't want to go to those strange places any more. But I couldn't tell it to anyone, not even to your father and grandmother. Who in his right mind would dare say anything? And what was the use of complaining? It was what you were expected to do, the duties and obligations you could not afford to evade.

As my mother's life and dreams were torn apart and tossed around, so was my family. In 1970, the fourth year into the Cultural Revolution, the Party called on urban cadres to settle down in rural areas to be reeducated by peasants and to reform themselves through labor. Mother, her identity now reduced to the spouse of a "reactionary" writer, was among the first to leave the city. She had been to different areas in the countryside many times, but this time she was supposed to settle down indefinitely. She was also ordered to have her city residential permit changed into a rural one and was expected to bring her children along. After pleading with the Revolutionary Committee in her work unit, the provincial library, mother was granted her request to take only her two younger children, my brother and me with her. My two older sisters, both in the middle school, were allowed to stay in the city with my grandmother.

Our family was thus split into three parts: my father was then hospitalized in a tuberculosis hospital in Chaohu County; my grandma and sisters were in Hefei; and my mother, my brother, and I were on our way to Lujiang, about two hundred miles south of Hefei. Our household belongings were also divided up. My mother brought along half of the furniture—a big wooden bed, an old brown five-drawer chest with an attached square mirror, a small redwood folding table, and two tall stools. The provincial library arranged for a truck to pick up our furniture, but we would have to travel on our own. First we had to cross a river, a tributary of Chaohu Lake, to get to a small town called Sanhe. From there we had to find space on the bus and ride for hours before we could arrive at the town center of Huangdao People's Commune, my mother's designated area of service. Finally, we would walk the rest of the twenty miles to get to the village where we would be staying.

On an early morning in June 1971, my mother, my younger brother, and I said good-bye to our grandma and sisters and boarded a ferry—a small fishing boat—at the quay in the eastern outskirts of Hefei. The boat was about three meters long and one meter wide. The boatman stood at the bow rowing with a pair of oars; my brother and I sat in the middle row of passenger's seats and my mother was at the stern. The sun was just rising from under the water, half of its face shining with brightened gold and half submerged in the deep orange tumbling rings that danced in a gentle river wind. Other small fishing boats resting in the quay were now awakening and preparing for a new day. Men were cleaning the decks and preparing fishing gear; women were repairing fishing nets and washing in the water; children, who all had water gourds tied on their backs, ran around on the deck. On the edge of most boats perched a black, sharp-beaked fish hawk, a leashed diving bird used by fishermen to catch fish. The fish hawk watched simultaneously with vigilant eyes any movement of fish under the water and of children on the boat. My brother and I waved to other children as our boat passed by theirs. They waved back, shouting something to us, their words lost in the splash of our boatmans' oars, cutting through the water, and in our mother's silence.

By the time we finally arrived at the village after five hours on the bus and another two on the road, dusk was approaching. One of the army personnel from my mother's work unit, the provincial library, was there to meet and introduce us to the production team leaders from Huangdao People's Commune. We were then led to a small thatched house standing alone at the entrance of the village. The discolored wooden door screeched like a wounded cat when being pushed open. The door frame was so low that all grown-ups had to stoop a little to get in. The inside of the house had about twenty square feet, with only one small window of wooden bars without glass. My mother later pasted a newspaper on the bars for a temporary windowpane. The rafters and tiles had gone up shortly before we came, the production team leader explained. The walls, made by compacting mud and stones between wooden separators, had not been whitewashed, and there was no ceiling. The dirt floor had bumps and holes here and there, like that of the unfinished bomb shelters I had been to in our city. In the corners of the room spiders were busy making their own homes, ignoring us newcomers. Our furniture—a five-drawer chest, a double bed, a small folding table, the two wooden stools—took much of the space. Crouched in one inner corner of the room was a white brick fire stove, which I later would call the "monster stove."

The villagers appeared to be kind and warm, although they looked puzzled and even pityingly at us, wondering what on earth this woman and her children were doing here. One of the young boys asked my brother if that army officer from the provincial library was our father. Without a word, my brother picked up a piece of dirt and threw it at him, screaming, "He is *your* father! Damn you!" The little boy was startled, looking both confused and hurt at this radical response to his simple question. Grabbing my brother's hands and pulling him over to her, mother apologized to the little boy. Afterward she warned both of us not to show any disrespect to any of these villagers, men or women, young or old.

"We are here to receive their reeducation, understand?"

No, we didn't understand, not at all. We didn't understand why we had to quit our school in the city and settle down in this small village; we didn't understand what it meant to receive reeducation from these villagers. One thing was clear to us, though: this was only one of those endless assignments and tasks my mother was obligated to fulfill. She would do it without complaining and with utter dedication.

So she did. Soon after we settled down in that dimly lit, dirt-floor house, my mother started working with the peasants in the paddy fields. Growing up a city girl, mother had never worked in the fields before. But she managed to learn how to plant seedlings, build paddy embankments, harvest grain, shovel manure, and carry buckets of water with a shoulder pole. Every morning before dawn, when the loudspeaker on the electric pole right beside our house blared the music of "The East Is Red and the Sun Rises," mother left for the field and came back around eight o'clock to prepare breakfast for my brother and me. She would leave and return for lunch and took off again before coming home after dark.

Left to ourselves most of the time, my brother and I went out and befriended other village children, who often took us on wild excursions to the fields or haystacks and around the village. But the fun would be over when mother returned. We had to go back to our shelter to be with our spider friends and to eat the dust that hovered in the air whenever we walked. For me, it was time to help mother fix supper on the white monster stove. Mother was not good at cooking, but she was even more hopeless when she had to cook on this big brick stove called a zao. It would take her a full hour just to start a fire with dry rice straw and cotton twigs. The smoke would start her coughing and make her eyes water. Once the fire started, I would sit on the brick bench behind the zao, feeding the fire with more straw and twigs to keep it going while mother stood in front, spilling rice into boiling water in a big iron wok or pouring some cabbage or other seasonal vegetables into the heated wok and stir-frying them. When she had a moment, she would relieve me by sitting down behind the stove and poking the fire with a long iron bar to make it stronger. By the time we finished cooking each meal, our faces were smeared with ashes and food stains, our hands bruised and burned from thorny cotton twigs and fire sparks.

Toward midsummer, it started raining incessantly for days on end. Mother, along with the other peasants, had to race against time to have the early season rice harvested and late season rice planted. One of her peasant friends gave her a big bamboo coat in the shape of a giant peanut shell, which she wore while planting seedlings in the rain. When she was home earlier than usual, we would sit together around our small red folding table, chatting and listening to the patter of the rain on the tiles above us. Occasionally, if she was in a good mood, mother would tell us a story or hum a song. Sometimes, she took us out to the field to look at the newly planted rice. It was wet everywhere. The grass along the road and the seedlings in the paddy fields grew taller and greener each day. Once, mother, holding a discolored oilcloth umbrella over us, pointed to the green paddy fields and said, "Look at these rice plants. How fast they have grown. We are just like rice, aren't we?" Then she turned to us and continued. "Yes, we are just like these rice plants. Mama will grow old and you'll grow up, right?" She then shook her head and heaved a sigh. "But we are not plants, are we? These plants do not have brains. And we do. What would you say, children?" Though not sure exactly what she meant, my brother and I nodded along, feeling her gentle touch on our heads and shoulders.

Toward the end of that summer, the rainfall became heavier and heavier. The river located at the east side of our village had risen to a dangerous level. The loudspeaker was warning that the dam could overflow at any time and asked the villagers to be prepared for flooding. Worried about our safety, mother asked for a leave of absence and took us back to Hefei to be with my grandma. She planned to return to the village two days later. The day before her scheduled departure from Hefei, a telegram arrived bringing us bad news that the river had flooded most of the village. Our house had collapsed and all the furniture had been either swept away or ruined.

Mother folded the telegram away and never mentioned it again. My grandmother started crying.

"What about now? Where are you going to live? Where are you going to live?" Mother raised her right hand and pulled all her dark brown hair back with an elastic band and started packing. "I must go," she said, "Please take care of the two little ones for me, Ma. I will be back soon."

The flood was disastrous. It destroyed most of the houses in the village as well as ours. When the flood receded, I went back to the village. I waded through the muddy water that reached up to my calves and tried to retrieve some of our belongings. The only piece of furniture left was the five-drawer chest, its lower half still immersed in the water and the rest covered with brownish and stinky mud, its mirror, unbroken, still shin-

ing. After much struggling, I managed to pry open two top drawers and took out their contents—clothing tangled with mud and water—and put them in a big linen bag I had borrowed from one of the villagers. I carried it to the office of the production team, a small brick house where I would stay temporarily along with all the other villagers, most of whom were women with young children and who cursed the flood and cried for their lost homes.

I didn't cry. From the moment I received the telegram to the time I joined the homeless villagers in that dank and fusty room, I didn't shed a single tear or utter a single word of complaint. No use complaining. Whatever and however you felt, you swallowed it up and smoothed it over. It was what you were supposed to do. That was all there was to it. If that was what you were assigned to do, you just had to do it because of your duties, your responsibility, and above all, your faith in and loyalty to the Party.

After that flood, mother insisted that brother and I stay in the city and go back to school, while she stayed in the village alone. She would come back home once a month, usually on a Saturday. It became our routine that my siblings and I would go straight from school on that particular Saturday to meet our mother at the quay. Each time when she walked toward us along that narrow swing bridge from the boat, her weary dusty face would glow into a smile.

Mother stayed in Lujiang for another year before she was finally allowed to be transferred to Chaohu county so as to be closer to my father, who had been staying at the tuberculosis hospital for over two years now. I visited mother in summer 1973 when she was working as a secretary in the office of the County Party Committee, helping with the archives and with other secretarial duties. The office where she worked, The Chaohu County Communist Party Committee, sat on the top of a hill called Hero Mountain. She lived at the foot of the hill in one of the small dorms inside a big walled courtyard. Everyday, she had to climb up a steep stone stairway as high as a ten-story building to get to work, and then down to return to her dorm.

Her room was small, like a matchbox into which was crowded a double bed covered with a thin bamboo mat, a desk that also served as a night stand, and a folding chair. In its innermost corner, on the other side of the bed, stood the faded green canvas suitcase that had accompanied my mother to her wedding. I stayed in the room during the daytime doing homework, and sometimes played in the courtyard with the neighbor's big brown dog. Mother, who had always been afraid of any animals, especially dogs, seemed to be fond of this one. "He is good company," mother said, "guarding my door whenever I am not around and greeting me whenever I come home."

As she said these words, her voice was a little choked as if with sobs. Holding my hands in hers, she let out a sigh. "It is so good to have you here," she often said to me. Sometimes after our supper, mother would take me to the top of the hill along the stone stairs winding through evergreen bushes on both sides. We often counted how many stairs altogether; sometimes we had eight hundred and other times we had more. Each time we reached the top I was breathless, panting, and had to sit on one of the stone lions that squatted at the end of the stairway. Mother would stand beside me, smiling, breathing as steadily as if she had been waiting for me at the top all along. She then would hold out her arms to me, with her palms spreading upward. It was a signal she always gave to us when we were younger so that we could follow and catch up with her on busy crowded streets. Feeling like a small child again, I put my hand in hers and we both walked toward an open space on the top of the hill where we watched the sun set and clouds coast by.

With the same calm and steady steps, mother walked through another three years before finally returning to the city and her home in the autumn of 1975. Twenty-two years had passed since she and my father had married on that rainy Saturday evening. When my mother and father stood together side-by-side beside the creek in the birch forest, holding on to their yellow oilcloth umbrella in a world of rain, they could not have known that rain would wash away the moments and the dreams they shared and the promises they made to themselves and to each other. For them, the clear raindrops falling upon the grass had turned into only a reflection of rainbow. But both eventually found their way back to their lost dreams and broken promises. For mother, these dreams and promises manifest themselves in each picture she draws, in each poem she writes, and in each song she sings.

Often, when I watch her painting, read her poems, or listen to her sing, I picture that twenty-year-old art student, wearing a gray double-breasted Lenin jacket, carrying a green canvas suitcase, her thick and long braids with sky-blue ribbon bows swaying at her waist, hurrying to her wedding in a warm spring rain. I always love to imagine what she would have looked like if she were dressed in a bright red qipao embroidered with a blooming peony and dancing phoenix.

I know she would be so beautiful, both then and now.

槐花 10

The Winter Solstice

It was the eve of Dongzhi *2004—the winter solstice, the time for the living to send blessed offerings to their beloved ones in another world to prepare them for a long and cold winter.*

Snowflakes fell silently from a lowering sky and a few stars sparkling, diamonds in the winter darkness—diamonds that seemed to mark a path for us across this world to the one beyond. Carrying with them matches and paper offerings—money, clothing, jewels—people embarked on this path, hoping to see, to talk, and to be with their loved ones on this snowy winter evening. They piled up their blessed offerings like pyramids in cemeteries, in the parks, or on the sidewalk; they struck matches and lit the fire. As those blessings went up in flame and the blazes brightened up the darkening sky, the smoke gave the cold and damp air a faintly burned odor that smelled like a breath of spring.

That evening in my parents' backyard, I was standing with my mother, sisters, and six-year-old daughter in front of our own pyramid.

My mother handed me a box of matches. "This year," she said, "You light the fire. You have been away every Dongzhi. *Now you are here. They will be so happy to see you."*

The match felt heavy in my hands as I listened to my mother's words. Yes, having been away from home for so many years, I had almost forgotten this ancient ritual through which we are expected to reach out to our ancestors, to meet and talk to them. It dawned on me that I might have missed many opportunities to be with my grandparents on this special day. Under the attentive gaze of ten eyes, I took a match from the match box, struck it, and lit the pile of the offerings. The flame went up higher and higher, forming a halo in which I first saw my Village Nainai *(my paternal grandma), and then my* City Nainai *(my maternal grandma). We nicknamed them for the sake of convenience since we referred to them both as nainai, meaning "grandma." Like that little match girl who sees her grandma in the heavens, I kept striking one match after another in order to see mine and hold them in my arms again and again. In the meantime, I heard my mother and sisters whispering, "Yeiyei, nainai, yeiyei (grandpa), nainai. Are you doing well there? Do you need anything else? Please tell us, please do. We miss you. Bless us, bless us, bless us."*

Anying, who had been watching quietly during the whole ritual, now grabbed and shook my arms and giggled. "Will yeiyei and nainai hear them?"

She looked up at me with her big clear eyes in which I could see flames dancing.

"Yes, they will. If you talk to them, they will hear you," I told her.

"Can they talk to us? Can we see them? Can we hear them?"

"Yes." I answered, and struck yet another match. The fire grew stronger and brighter; the air became alive and warm with dancing snowflakes and swirling ashes. I looked up at the sky, letting snowflakes and ashes fall on my face, feeling their gentle touch, knowing that the touch came from above, from my two dear grandmothers who were watching us right now, amazed by how their grandchildren and great-grandchildren had grown—out of them and for them.

Both of my grandmothers were born around the year 1910. Both entered prearranged marriages at the age of seventeen or eighteen and carried from that time on the burden of taking care of their husbands and children. They both had one daughter and two sons, although my aunt, my father's sister, had died as an infant. They were about the same height, and wore the same traditional woman's outfit, a dajinshan, made of blue cloth which had a side-opening with buttons lining up along the left side in the shape of "S." They both kept long hair to the waist and made it into a bun behind the nape of their necks. While my Village Nainai used only a black hair net to hold her bun, my City Nainai fastened hers with both a jade hair pin and an ivory comb. The most conspicuous difference between my two nainais, however, would be their feet.

My City Nainai had a pair of what was called "three-inch golden Lotus feet." Most young girls who lived in cities had their feet bound, which served the practical purpose of securing a good marriage. In most cases, this was arranged by their parents and match-makers, and it was rare that the husband and wife-to-be would actually meet each other before marrying and spending the rest of their lives together. For most grooms, the wedding night would be the first time they got to see their brides. These brides' faces would be covered with red head scarves and the rest of their bodies robed in long wedding gowns. The only visible part was their feet, which if they were small and elegant, like a pair of lotuses, would speak well indeed of the delicate womanly beauty of the bride.

To ensure that their daughter and granddaughter married well, City Nainai's mother and grandmother became close allies. Every evening before my grandma went to bed, her mother and grandma would work as a team: one grabbed her arms to keep her from moving while the other wrapped strips of cloth tightly over her feet layer by layer. She begged them not to, with both tears and screams, but her mother and grandma continued. Despite the painful weight they had to bear walking on their own tiny bound feet, they wrapped her feet, blind and deaf to her tears and pleadings, believing they were doing her a favor. In the night she couldn't sleep, my grandma told us, her feet swelling up inside thick layers of cloth, itching and burning with pain.

Consequently, my City Nainai suffered all her life from the pain and inconvenience these bound feet inflicted on her. We didn't get to see her feet often since she wore socks all the time. At the end of each day after she had finished all the household chores, my grandma would pour herself a big basin of hot water, take off her socks, and soak her feet in the water. Her face contorted with agony as her feet touched the steaming water which was, she said through clenched teeth, the only way to relieve that itch and pain. After that, she would let out a deep sigh, close her eyes for a moment, and then wrap her feet with a dry towel and put on clean socks. She usually carried out this routine after we went to bed, but a few times we peeped into her basin and were horrified to see a pair of disfigured flesh balls of which we could hardly tell apart the toes, backs, arches, or the rest of her feet.

While my City Nainai had to endure this pain of foot-binding in the name of marriage and beauty, my Village Nainai was spared this torture for an equally practical yet different reason: she had to work in the fields from a very young age, helping her stepparents with farm work. Although she was about the same height as my City Nainai, my Village Nainai's feet were double the size of my City Nainai's. We chuckled whenever we saw their two pairs of shoes put together, tiny boats next to big ships ready any time to sail. Riding on this big ship, my Village Nainai sailed through the open fields, planting and harvesting rice, wheat, corn, sweet potatoes, and vegetables, taking care of her husband, three children, and the household. Though about the same age as my City Nainai, my Village Nainai looked much older. Frequent exposure to the sun and rough wind had left its marks on her dry and wrinkled face and her brown brittle hair. But her overall build was stronger than that of my City Nainai, the strength obviously accentuated by her big feet which carried her like wind when she walked.

In the southern part of our province where my father grew up, women did all the fieldwork. The men—heads of their households—either sauntered around the fields or stayed at home. A few would work only at "highly skilled fieldwork" such as plowing, a comparatively comfortable but, as they claimed, more complicated job because how well one could handle the tilling implements determined how wide and deep one could plow the field, which would have a definite impact on the crop yield. Besides, it was a traditional belief that women should not touch or be anywhere near cattle. It would bring bad luck to the earth which, in its revenge, would remain barren.

Having established these rules, the men wouldn't deign to do anything else. Since plowing needed only a few people, most of these men just idled, playing poker, having tea, and telling stories. My yeiyei, for one, never bothered to go out to work in the fields all his life. Neither did he offer to help my grandma with any household chores such as cooking and cleaning. To use his and other men's words, these were all women's jobs. In his family, all work was my grandma's duty, both outside and inside.

Becoming an orphan at the age of four, my grandma was adopted by my grandpa's family in the neighboring village as a tongyangxi, a future daughter-in-law. Her fiancé, my future grandpa who was about five years her senior, was then going to a private village school. How envious she was when watching the boy learn to read and write, nainai used to tell us, whereas she had to learn how to cook for the family, how to plant vegetables, how to spin yarn, how to feed pigs, how to raise chicks, ducks, and geese, and how to fetch water from the village well with wooden buckets and then carry them home on a shoulder pole. She didn't mind these chores since she loved being outdoors in the sun and the air, but she also wanted to learn to read and write, which was virtually impossible for her to do at the time.

When they were married—at the ages of sixteen and twenty-one, respectively—my grandma officially took the family name Lu and with it the burden of taking care of the family. In the following five years they had three children, two boys and one girl. My father was the oldest, the first son. As soon as he reached school age, my grandma insisted on sending him to the only school in the village and relentlessly rejected my grandfather's proposal that the boy stay home and help out with the fieldwork. My father often told us that one of his fondest memories of his mother was how, on the first day of each fall semester, which always followed the harvest, she would carry on a bamboo shoulder pole a pair of round wicker baskets of freshly shelled rice to the teacher for my father's tuition. Despite the heavy weight that curved both ends of the shoulder pole, my grandma still managed to keep her steps fast and steady. She would then in a clear and firm voice tell the teacher, an old-fashioned scholar dressed in a traditional Chinese gown, "He is all yours, xiansheng (the honorific for a teacher). Do whatever you can to teach him. If he doesn't study hard, you punish him. Have no mercy!"

She herself did whatever she could to let her son study. She would never allow him to help her with any of the household chores or the fieldwork. To let my father read without having to worry about light, she stored a large quantity of lamp oil which she bought from the village store with the money she earned by selling duck and chicken eggs. My grandfather, seeing the lamp burning late in the night, often complained about wasting too much oil and ordered his son to put off the light and go to bed. But my grandma, though rarely contradicting her husband, would insist that her son finish whatever he had been reading or writing, assuring him that there would always be enough oil. No matter how late my father studied, she would keep him company, sitting quietly in the corner, spinning yarn or sewing shoes and clothes.

My father didn't disappoint his mother. He became the top student and pride of the merciless teacher, who told my grandma how intelligent my father was and what a terrible waste it would be if he stayed in the village without further pursuing his study in middle and high school. Knowing how expensive it was to go to the county seat for high school, my father chose to stay in the village, helping his mother with fieldwork and taking care of his younger brother while continuing to read voraciously on his own. When he was about fourteen or fifteen, my grandma suggested that he take the entrance exam for high school. She told him not to worry about the money, that she had earned and saved enough for him to go. My father took tests for a couple of schools and got high scores on all of them, but none of these schools would accept him on the grounds that he didn't have an official diploma from an elementary and middle school. My grandma wouldn't allow her son to give up. She accompanied him to all the schools near and far, in the whole county, covering hundreds and hundreds of miles and wearing out at least three pairs of homemade cloth shoes. She was never tired; her feet seemed to carry them through the rough hills and rugged country roads until my father was finally admitted as a special case into one of the best high schools in Chaohu county.

That was my grandma, walking like wind, riding on her sailing ships in the fields, and to the city, to us. My parents often recalled with gratitude how, when each of us girls was born, my grandmother would come to visit, carrying on a shoulder pole two bamboo baskets full of hens, eggs, and other produce. When my brother was born in the early 1960s, the beginning of one of the worst famines in the nation's history, food was rationed in the cities and was scarce in rural areas. There was nothing for her to bring. Everyone in the village was going hungry and many were dying. She herself was weak and frail, having nothing to eat but watery porridge and dried sweet potato strips. But my grandma was determined to see her newly born grandson. By that time, all the railways were closed, and the trains were no longer transporting passengers in order to prevent famished peasants from flooding into the city. My grandma decided that she would walk. She risked her life by hitting the road with little in her stomach not eating for several days and trekked for almost two hundred miles along the railway from predawn to dusk. She finally made it to Hefei with a giddy head and shaking legs, just as she made it many other times in the following years, to visit us as we grew older.

She would come twice a year—after the fall harvest ended and before the spring ploughing began. Each time she visited, she would bring the food us city kids could only dream of. She was always carrying a linen sack on her back and holding a bamboo basket on her right arm. In the sack and basket were a variety of treasures. There was fresh produce she had planted and harvested: fresh peanuts, sweet potatoes, hens she had raised herself, and of course chicken, duck, and goose eggs. There were home-made snacks too: rice cakes, peanut candy cakes, and sesame candy cakes. My Village Nainai spoke little, but when she did, she was always urging us to eat or drink something. She enjoyed the company of my City Nainai, both of them often sat face-to-face chatting, listening to each other, smiling, and occasionally bursting into a hearty laughter. However, none of her visits would last more than two weeks. Then she became restless, eager to return to the village. Whenever my father tried to persuade her to stay a little longer, my grandma just shook her head and smiled, "Here I can't walk too far. My feet get itchy." My father often said that his mother's feet would walk like wind only in an open field.

By the spring of 1976, when I settled down in the village in response to Mao's call to receive reeducation from peasants, my grandma was already in her early seventies. Her back was now slightly hunched, her wrinkles had turned into deep furrows, and her hair was all gray, but her feet seemed to be as strong as ever, carrying her to the fields where she picked cotton, watered vegetables, planted and gathered rice. I lived with two other students in a room assigned to us by the production team, the basic unit of the People's Commune, but went to my grandparents' for both lunch and supper. Whenever I could, I offered to help with the chores, but my grandma would not even let me near the kitchen. "Do something you like, Sanzi," she would say. "Like your father, go and grab something to read, I like to hear you reading." And that was what we did lots of times when we were both at home during the winter and rainy evenings.

On those snowy or rainy nights, when there wasn't much to do in the field, my grandma would sit on her bamboo chair at her old wooden spinning wheel, her right hand swiveling its handle, her left hand reeling out as if by magic endless lengths of yarn from a small cotton ball. I would sit on a lower stool across from her, reading and listening to the musical rhythm of the spinning wheel. Every now and then when I looked up from my book at her, her eyes would meet mine and we would both smile. All the time she was weaving, her hands reeled and rolled while her feet rested firmly on the earth floor, ready to sail.

Standing on her three-inch lotus feet, my City Nainai was as strong as she was beautiful. She had a wide shining forehead and deep calm but knowing eyes. Her abundant velvet dark hair, coiled into a chignon with an elegant ivory comb, was always shining with the oil she applied, oil that had the fresh scent of rain-washed spring air. That fresh scent came from a small crystal bottle shaped like a swan. It perched on the back right corner of a brown five-drawer chest in our bedroom. Beside the swan bottle was a small round metal box, with two enamel orioles singing under a deep blue sky. It was her favorite face cream and smelled like fruit candy. For all her endless household chores, my City Nainai kept herself clean and poised; her steps were light and steady, carrying with them a pleasant rhythm in whatever she did and wherever she went.

My maternal grandparents lived with their two sons, my uncles, in a city about four hundred miles away from ours. When my mother gave birth at twenty-one to my oldest sister in 1954, my grandma came to live with my mother, taking care of the baby and the household. She stayed on afterward, watching over one after another as each grandchild was born and protecting us with her warm wings during the most turbulent years.

In my childhood memory, my City Nainai seemed to work around the clock—cooking meals, cleaning the house, making snacks, cutting and sewing clothes and shoes, watching us do our homework, tucking us in and telling us bedtime stories. Every day after we returned home from school, a big pot of steamed buns was waiting for us. When wheat flour was rationed because of a severe food shortage, she substituted corn and sweet potato flour, which she magically turned into small delicious conical and oval golden rolls. For the Chinese New Year Festival, she made dumplings and bread which came in different sizes and shapes: rabbits, squirrels, porcupines, fish, and dragons. For the Mid-Autumn Festival, she kneaded and baked mooncakes with beautiful magpies and peach trees carved on both sides. For the Dragon and Lantern Festival, she wrapped glutinous rice in dried bamboo leaves with a filling of red bean paste. If any one of us was sick, she would cook a special dish, noodle or dough-drop soup, sprinkling on the top a few slices of golden yolk, green onion, and a few drops of amber-colored sesame oil. Watching the lucky one sip the hot soup and blow its surface into happy circles, we all wished we could get sick.

My grandma, however, tried her best to prevent sickness from happening. At a time when we were left practically without either of our parents around, she made sure that we were as healthy as we could be, both physically and psychologically. She filled our stomachs with sweet goodies and delicious meals; she kept our bodies warm with the cotton-padded jackets and cloth shoes she sewed; she nurtured our minds with beautiful stories and magic tales she told under starry nights and around the warm stove fire.

Even compared with all those tales of beautiful and witty spirits, immortals, and fairies, I liked her own story the best, told in a plain and sometimes painful tone, narrated to herself as much as to us in a simple, clear sketch—her girlhood, her marriage, her own family, and the other family she helped to raise. Like my Village Nainai, she married my grandfather at a young age, seventeen, in a union previously arranged by a matchmaker. My grandfather was the only son in his family, so my grandma bore the burden of giving birth to boys who could carry on the family name.

Four years later, after having twin daughters first, my grandma had two sons, thus more or less securing her position in the Zhang family. But before long, she was burdened with another family, a much bigger one, that of her sister-in-law. My grandfather had one sister who had married young into a family of higher social status and within seven years had six sons. Her husband was a business man who spent most of his time away from home. Then one day, although nobody could pinpoint a specific time, she seemed to have lost herself somewhere in a world unknown to those around her. At first she forgot to get up, to cook, or to do any of the household chores. It was as if she was always in a trance. Then she started going out, her hair uncombed and tangled, her face pale and bland. She was always murmuring something nobody could understand.

"Only I could." Grandmother said. "She was murmuring the name of someone she could have married." My grandmother was the only one who knew the man with whom her sister-in-law had fallen deeply in love but couldn't marry since she was already engaged to the Tong family. Not long after her youngest son was born, she told my grandma that she had seen the man somewhere in the city. My grandma said it was impossible because that man lived in her sister-in-law's hometown, which was hundreds of miles away. But her sister-in-law insisted that she had seen him and started babbling that she was going to find him and maybe marry him. "He was the one I should have married," she told my grandma.

So she went out, leaving behind her six young boys at home crying for their mother. She would wander in the city for the whole day and return home before dark. Eventually, all the neighbors assumed that she was demented for reasons they didn't understand. Time went by quietly until one day when she was seen running naked in a pouring rain on one of the busiest streets. Cold rain drops slashed her face and whipped her body, but she kept running, as if chasing someone only she could see.

As soon as the news reached the house, my grandmother went out immediately to find her, covered her with an overcoat, and dragged her back home. She was shivering in my grandma's arms, hysterically laughing and crying. Then she fell into a long heavy sleep. The next morning, her fate was determined for her: she was to be sent to a mental institution. The Tong family wouldn't tolerate such shameful behavior and wanted nothing to do with her. My grandmother and grandfather took her out of the house and committed her to the clinic. When they were about to leave, my great aunt burst out sobbing. Holding my grandma's hands, she knelt down in front of her. "The boys," she cried choked with tears. "The boys, the boys." My grandma held her arms and lifted her up. "Don't worry about the boys. I will take good care of them. Don't worry about them. I promise. I promise."

My grandma kept her promise, faithfully and lovingly. She took in her sister-in-law's six sons and raised them as her own even after their father remarried. Their stepmother wouldn't take in her husband's children. What happened to her sister-in-law? She ran away from that clinic three months later and nobody ever saw her afterward. My grandma tried to search for her in the following years, but had no success, didn't even know if she was still alive or not.

"Poor sister! Six sons. Six. Never got to see them grow up. If heaven has eyes, she could at least find her man. But Ayaya," my grandma shook her head as if to negate any possibility. "No, no use. Whose fault was it that we were born women? What can you do then? Whatever the bitterness and sorrow, you eat and swallow it. What else can you do, uh? What can you do? If you married someone, you lived with him for good. You can't change that. Who knew our husbands before marrying them? No one did. I was lucky to have someone like your grandfather. Not everyone would have this luck. Like your great aunt. It was worse that she already had someone before marrying. But it is a different time now. Look at your mama and baba; they met and married all on their own. You girls are lucky."

She is right. We *are* lucky—because of her ever present love and care. Among my siblings, I might be the luckiest one. Had it not been for my grandma, I could have become a tiny baby skeleton who wouldn't have grown to see the sunrise beyond the first year.

At the age of eleven or twelve months, I was suddenly stricken by a high fever and dark red rashes all over the skin. My father was staying in a hotel at the west end of the city working on his new film script, and my mother was at work. My City Nainai, not knowing how to call an ambulance and having no phone handy, somehow managed to get on the right bus, find the hotel, then after a fierce argument with the door guard, who initially forbade her to enter but soon gave in, raced to my father's room and yelled at the top of her lungs, "How could you stay here writing, uh? Sanzi is dying! She is dying! You come home with me now, right now!" My father first was stunned then panicked. He dialed 119 and called for an ambulance and then rushed home with my grandma.

When the paramedics arrived at my house, they could tell right away that I had scarlet fever, an often lethal infectious disease among infants. They ordered that the house immediately be disinfected. White-gowned doctors and nurses gave everyone present a gauze mask as they got ready to spray. When they started pumping white fog all over the house, the strong odor of disinfectant was so irritating that it hurt even through the masks. My grandma, however, refused to wear her mask; instead, she approached the nurses, trying to grab those sprayers while crying: "The child is not dead yet. What you are doing, uh? Why are you spraying the house? How can the baby breathe?" Two nurses had to hold her back and explain what they were doing. After a while, she calmed down, though still suspicious of those white-gowned men and women. Standing close beside my crib, she focused her eyes on their every move with the vigilance of a mother bird guarding her chick.

After that incident, my father developed a special attachment to me. Whenever people teased about my being my father's favorite daughter, my father would tell the story how my grandma broke into his hotel room and saved my life. My grandma, on the other hand, would simply smile and say, "You are a lucky girl."

I am lucky indeed, having been loved and nurtured by my grandma as I grew up and entered womanhood. Before that hot July noon, I was totally in the dark about what would happen to my body at a certain age. The female body and sexuality were absolutely forbidden topics throughout my childhood, teen years, and early adulthood. My mother never talked about it, nor did anyone at school. Public health classes had been canceled long before I entered middle school. Any topic concerning women's bodies were considered disgusting and shameful. I overheard some of my classmates making fun of and even bad-mouthing one of the girls who they said was "wearing bloody gloves" as if she had committed a horrible crime.

And whenever the word yuejing, period, came up in the few remaining health programs on radio stations, all us girls would cover our ears as if the very word would make us dirty.

So on that hot and humid July noon, when I woke up from a short nap on the cool bamboo bed to find myself sitting in a pool of blood, I thought I was going to die, either from bleeding or from some unknown disease that had suddenly fallen upon me. I started shaking and screaming, tears rolling down my cheeks into the dark thick blood. My grandma, who was then pasting cloth to make soles for our shoes, ran into the bedroom, her hands still covered with the sticky flour used as paste. The minute I saw her, my shrieks turned into suppressed weeping, as if instinctively I knew something terrible had happened to me. "I am bleeding, nainai," I muttered, my face burning red, my eyes avoiding that disgusting pool of liquid.

For a moment, my grandma seemed to be frozen, but quickly came to herself, nervously rubbing her hands back and forth before she approached me and held my hands in hers. "Oh, good heavens, good heavens." She seemed to whisper to herself, "It came. It came." She never explained what *it* was, but the fact that she knew *it* and the soothing tone she used to say *it* settled me down immediately and made me realize that it was not something I should be afraid or ashamed of.

My grandma then rushed back to the kitchen, put down the clothes and soles, washed her hands, and returned to our bedroom. She went straight to the chest, her hands fluttering up and down in the upper and lower drawers while telling me not to move. In just about a second, she changed into a clean blue dajing shirt and handed me a set of a short-sleeved blouse and dark colored pants. Helping me put on the clothing, she took up my hands and whispered to me, "Now, we have to go out. To buy something for you." I hesitated, not sure if I heard it right. To go out meant we would leave our complex and go into the streets. For my grandma, that was a major adventure. As far as I remembered, she had never been out of the complex. Whenever she needed some errand done like buying a pack of cigarettes or a bottle of soy sauce or vinegar, one of us four children would do it for her. The reason, of course, was that her feet simply couldn't take her far. The farthest she ever went was to the neighbors who lived next to us or a few doors down.

"Where are we going? Nainai? Can you go?" I asked, wondering how she would walk through crowded streets with her bound feet under the scorching July sun. But she already pulled me out of the door and locked it behind her. Her steps were small but fast. I could hardly follow her. I never knew she could ever walk with that speed as if something was pushing her from behind. Big drops of sweat broke out on her forehead; the back of her dajing shirt was all wet. Always particular about being tidy and clean, my grandma now didn't in the least care that she was sweating profusely. In a hurry to take me out, she didn't even carry with her a white embroidered handkerchief as she usually did to wipe clean her hair and face.

We wove our way through the throng of people, bicycles, and wheelbarrows and entered a dark-red four-story building—the biggest department store in the city. Once we got in, my grandma stopped as if she didn't know where to go. Then she went to the closest glass counter and whispered to the saleswoman who was sorting out some items from the cabinet. She looked up at me for a brief moment and then told my grandma something as she pointed her finger at another counter. Without saying anything to me, my grandma took my hands and the next thing I knew we were in front of a glass counter with a big red sign "Women's Necessities." My grandma again whispered to the saleswoman behind the counter— luckily for us, not many people were in the store—and again the woman turned around to look at me. It was hard to tell her expression, though. Bending over and reaching into the lower level of one of the glass cabinets, she grabbed a small package and handed it to my grandma. With visible relief, my grandma took the package from the woman's hands, thanked the woman over and over again and pulled me away from the counter.

That small package contained my first sanitary belt, a pink rubber belt two inches wide with two elastic straps affixed at each end to hold the straw paper. After each time that "old friend" paid me a visit, I would wash the belt very carefully and store it away until next time. I used it as long as I could, until one day the rubber belt broke and split up altogether. But I still cleaned it up and wrapped it over with a soft old handkerchief and placed it in the back corner of the bottom drawer of my dresser. After that first sanitary belt, I used many and discarded each one of them after a few months' use, but I never had the heart to throw away this very first one. Faithfully, it accompanied me through my teen years to adulthood, a quiet reminder of the presence of my grandma under whose rain and sunshine I grew.

Now I am a grown woman. Both of my grandmothers have passed away. My City Nainai left us on a chilly spring morning in 1985, fifteen years after her husband of forty years died during the ravaging revolutionary storm. She had been bedridden for years, more mentally and physically drained as each day went by. On a sunny March morning, the day before she died, grandma struggled to get out of the bed, her face looking somewhat refreshed and even beaming. She said she was feeling much better and wanted to have a bath. My mother knew how she liked to keep clean and found it hard to deny her wish. After her bath, she put on one of her best blue dajing shirts and sat on a bamboo chair near the window in the early spring sunlight. My father made her a special dish—stir-frying a whole fish, qiuanyu, which is pronounced the same as the phrase for "full discovery." She ate almost half of it. Her face was pale, almost lucent under the white sun, peaceful and calm. A faint smile lingered at the corner of her eyes as she squinted at the sun. That night, she went to bed and fell into a sleep from which she never woke up.

My Village Nainai lived longer. When she reached her eighties and couldn't do any fieldwork, she finally agreed to come to the city and live with us. When I left China for Canada in the spring of 1991, the whole family went to the train station to see me off, including my then eighty-five-year-old grandma. She had lost her hearing by that time, and her eyes could hardly see beyond one meter ahead, but she was still physically fit and still walked like wind, only a bit slower. The train started moving. Each figure receded farther and farther. Gazing on her tiny frail body and her fluttering white hair, I burst into tears at the thought that this might be the last time I would ever see her.

Four years later, she could still stand on her feet in front of our gate to greet my homecoming, despite her hunched back and a walking cane. I rushed to her side and embraced her small and fragile body. She could hardly see me or hear me, having lost both her sight and her hearing, but her arms still felt strong as they held mine.

In the spring of 1998, I returned home with my six-month-old baby girl, Anying. As soon as I stepped into the house with the baby in my arms, accompanied by my parents and sisters who picked me up at the airport, I saw my grandma standing right beside the door, smiling, with her arms reaching out to take over the baby as if she had been waiting for this very moment all along. Her touch awakened Anying, who had been asleep all the way from the airport to home. She now opened her eyes wide, first looked at her great-grandmother with curiosity, and then flashed a toothless smile. My grandma returned it with her own toothless smile. The two seemed to communicate in their own secret language.

During the three months I stayed at home, my grandma got up early every morning and sat in the living room right beside the crib, waiting for her turn to rock it while the baby was taking her morning nap. As I listened to the wooden crib swinging back and forth with a steady rhythm flowing from under my grandma's feet, I remembered those quiet winter evenings when she sat beside her spinning wheel, her feet resting firmly on the earth floor and her hands magically growing a strong and endless yarn that seemed never to break.

Six months later, my daughter and I boarded the train to Shanghai from where we would fly to the U.S. Despite my parents' and siblings' efforts to keep her at home, my grandma, Village Nainai, insisted on seeing us off at the railway station. I locked myself in her arms as long as I could, touching and being touched by her. I knew that was all I needed to take with me, the touch that would penetrate my body, reaching into my soul, giving me the strength I needed to move onward. Then I took my steps, as my City Nainai and Village Nainai had walked before me.

I didn't look back. I know she was watching me, and so was my City Nainai.

It was deep into evening now. The flame was now all gone.

Snowflakes and ashes were still fluttering up and down through the dark winter sky where stars were shining. Stars that lead our way to the path through which we get to be with those whom we love and who love us.

The winter solstice/dongzhi—the winter has arrived, touching us with its tender and warm blessings from the other world, bringing a welcome flavor of spring.

I held my daughter's hands and whispered into the snowing sky:

"Good night, Grandmas!"

I know they can hear me.

Sunset

It was July of the year 1970. The sun, searing the sky all day with its raging blaze, now looked down at the brown and barren land with a triumphant smile. The land, scorched of its last drop of moisture, twisted in anguish, breathing painfully through numerous cracked lips. Its vast brown surface was bisected in the middle by a narrow mud road which snaked like a dusty river from a gray concrete four-story building looming at the other end to where the sun was finally setting. Then the road came to a sudden stop in front of a low-roofed, windowless house before it disappeared beneath the earth without a trace.

Over this dusty river of a road, two shadows were floating slowly from the gray building toward the deep orange skyline. One was a tall man in his early forties who wore a blue-and-white-striped patient shirt and pants and dragged his legs along with the help of heavy wooden crutches. He had a wan face and weary eyes and looked emaciated. Beside him was a little girl who walked with a bouncing gait, her two long pigtails swaying in the windless heat. Their steps were surrounded by a deep silence, broken only by the cracking sound of the dirt under their feet and the dull echo of the wooden crutches, slowly yet persistently pounding the dry patches of the earth.

They continued their silent walk toward the burning horizon until the only company in the vast wilderness—that windowless house—moved into their range of vision. They stopped about twenty yards away from the house, as if taking precautions not to step into its territory. They looked around, sat down on some massive boulder or just by the roadside to rest. All the while they felt they were being watched by that silent and gloomy face staring vacantly at them, its eye—a colorless wooden door—squinting at something they couldn't see. After a few minutes, they would resume their journey back toward that gray hospital where the air stank of a mixture of phenol, Lysol, and blood.

It had been a month now since I left my grandmother and my siblings at home and joined my father in this isolated rural area, about two hundred miles from the city where I lived. He was here because he needed medical treatment for his end-stage tuberculosis. I was here to keep him company, as I had been longing to do ever since he left home. I had been begging and pleading with my parents and grandma to allow me to spend the summer with my father. I persuaded them with the fact that, since I had battled through tuberculosis at the age of seven and was thus immune to it, they had nothing to worry about. Nothing else made me feel more secure than being with my father, even if it meant to live with fear among the sick and dying, to witness with despair their often futile struggle to stay alive.

As if knowing it couldn't escape from the heavy shadow of death, the hospital chose to hide itself in this rural wilderness where the air was stagnant and the land was sterile. It was a place where nothing would rise except the steam sizzling from the yellow earth, a place where nobody wanted to stay except those who were dead or dying. The hospital had two entrances, like a pair of snake eyes, one in the wall that served as its front and the other in its back. While the back eye, a narrow wooden door, looked fearfully into the wilderness, the front one, a double frosted glass door, gazed longingly upon a paved road leading to a small bus station where a bus arrived about twice a day, morning and late afternoons, loading and unloading a handful of visitors whose faces were as pale and dusty as the road they had just traveled. They were temporary passersby who often left in a hurry, as if any delay here would prevent them from leaving at all. Those who chose to stay, like me, tried the best we could to battle our own fears that at any time we might lose our loved ones.

For me, this deep-rooted fear released itself into the silent empty wilderness as my father and I walked out of his sickroom, through the dim stark corridor, across the narrow wooden backdoor, and onto this dusty road winding toward the west. All that nerve-rattling noise—the clinking between bottles, the impatient yelling from exhausted nurses, the painful groaning from half-conscious patients, and the desperate screams from their relatives—now receded as we waded through the river of dust farther and farther away from hospital. We would walk on until we saw that sullen solitary house. We would then stop, and sit down on the roadside or some boulders nearby, resting for a while before turning around and taking off again.

Today, however, we seemed to have stayed much longer. Father hadn't moved at all for the last twenty minutes or so, his eyes still focusing on that lonely house in the wilderness. His crutches, lying forgotten beside him, waited quietly for his signal to move. Those crutches were the result of my grandfather's one week nonstop waffling, sawing, wattling, and hammering. After he had finished them, my grandfather painted on each one a dancing dragon. He wished these dragons would bring my father some good luck—in this case, the ability to walk on his own. But before my grandfather had the chance to see any of the luck bestowed upon his favorite son-in-law, he abruptly ended his own life as if he had foreseen what would befall my father. He chose to go down the road where he would be spared all the pain of watching it happen.

But the rest of us had watched. I was watching every day now how my father struggled with every step and with every breath. As I watched that frail and haggard figure, shivering like a withered leaf in the blistering sun, I was trying to remember when was the last time that I saw him as a tall and handsome man with broad shoulders and a straight back: the man who had endless stories and jokes to tell to his children and his friends, lots and lots of them; the man whose resonating laughter would shake the roof and walls; the man who would travel on foot through the deep mountain regions for months with only a brown travel bag on his back, visiting, interviewing, and writing about poverty-stricken peasants; the man who loved composing and reciting poems with an enchanting cadence.

But that enchanting voice was gone, silenced and sealed. So was his soul, which in its hopelessness to function on it own, thrust its despair into the body, shattering that body into pieces that could only be seen in his now slightly hunched back, slumped shoulders, thinning and ruffled gray hair, his ashen face with two sickly pink cheekbones, and his half-paralyzed legs. Where had he gone? That young, vibrant, charming, energetic father of four, that vigorous and ambitious bright novelist and playwright, that kind and generous friend of so many—where did he go? I couldn't and didn't want to remember. All I knew or cared to know was that he was still alive and I was with him. Nothing else would matter now.

By 1970, father had been on crutches for almost two years. Around the end of 1968, he was sent home on a stretcher after he injured his lower back carrying two baskets of bricks on a shoulder pole in the labor camp. The injury soon extended to his lower body, causing an excruciating pain in both legs. Before long, he couldn't even walk. Lying in bed for several months, he struggled to stand up, with the crutches my grandfather made for him. Many of his doctor friends came to see him and suggested that he try various mixtures of Chinese herbal medicines—the only medical consultation he could hope for. The hospitals during that time had developed a special kind of political awareness that made them vigilant of which patients they would accept and treat. My father had been cast into a category of a reactionary intellectual, thus a "demon monster" and didn't deserve their services. He tried whatever his doctor friends recommended and even made for him, but as each day went by, the pain and stiffness of the legs wouldn't go away; they only deteriorated.

The worst fear, of course, as predicted by many of these doctor friends, was that the damaged bones would eventually lead to a paralysis of the whole body. This horrifying prospect forced my parents to seek any possible treatment, however desperate. One of his friends recommended a private doctor who was said to possess certain traditional medicines passed down to him by his ancestors who were known for their skills in treating bone diseases. This private doctor, however, lived in a small rural town in Jiangsu Province, about three hundred miles south of Hefei. My father, though allowed to be home, was forbidden to go anywhere outside the city, not to mention outside the province. But after considerable negotiation with the Revolutionary Committee, with the help of one sympathetic member, my father was given a month off to visit the doctor.

The night before my parents' departure, my two sisters stayed up late knitting two pairs of stockings to keep father's legs warm. My brother and I didn't go to bed until midnight, just listening to our parents chatting. For the first time in years, my father's face seemed to light up, although his cheeks were unusually red. Occasionally he would burst into violent coughing and his breathing sounded heavy and labored, but we were too excited to notice these symptoms. The very thought of my father returning to us, walking on his own, laughing and telling stories as he used to, kept me awake all night.

On an early February morning my father, supported by his crutches and with the help of my mother and my sisters, got on board the southbound train. As the train's shrill whistle trailed off and the cloud of steam drifted away into the pale blue and orange skyline, we turned around, my sisters, brother, and I, holding each other's hands, bouncing and skipping our way out of the railway station into the warm and delightful early spring sunshine. Before we even had time to savor this rare welcome sunshine, we were thrown back into an even more threatening darkness. In less than a week, my parents returned home, with my father still hanging hopelessly on his crutches and my mother beside him, her face pale, her eyes red and swollen.

There was nothing my parents could do now.

During a routine test before the surgery, my father was found to have a more serious condition, a more horrifying disease—and in its late stage too—tuberculosis, a disease that was as deadly at the time as cancer is nowadays. He was constantly coughing and often vomited blood after a spasm of coughs. He became thinner and thinner; his body seemed to have shrunk, shaking with silent irregular rhythm. For fear that he would indeed die, or worse, give the disease to others, the Revolutionary Committee had him sent in early April 1970 to this epidemic hospital located in the most secluded area in Chaohu county, a hospital where all the patients had tuberculosis and most of them were just waiting to die.

Now, three months later, I was sitting with him. The sun was sinking further down into the waves of red and golden clouds. Soon we would have to go back to the hospital. Father didn't move, his eyes still locked with that mysterious one-eyed house which was watching him with a gloomy silence in return. It seemed that both were engaged in a silent conversation, a secret conversation that was not meant to be heard by anyone else besides themselves.

And then the silent conversation was interrupted by an outburst of violent coughing. Father's right hand reached into his pants pocket to fetch a handkerchief to cover his mouth. My mother had prepared many handkerchiefs for him, all of them white, and some of them embroidered with red, purple, blue, and yellow thread in tiny flower petals and stars. The one he took out this time had lilacs with a few green leaves in between. As he removed the handkerchief from his mouth, I could see that it was streaked with blood, the blood that had stained all of my dreams I had ever since my father left home for this hospital. In those dreams, blood was everywhere, trickling down the wall, streaming through the roof, flooding over the house, merging with the glowing twilight of the setting sun, and flowing back toward me, a river of blood. Floating on the surging waves of this river of blood was a black and lidless coffin in which my father's body lay in a cloud of darkness. I don't remember how many times I cried myself awake, my eyes swollen with cold tears and my throat sore from a burning scream.

Now that I was here with my father, those harrowing dreams seemed to have disappeared, yet they were replaced by a deeper anxiety and fear over the seemingly losing battle—his and those of many other patients I met in the hospital—and I couldn't see much hope.

Most of the patients here were from nearby rural areas and were the labor force needed in the fields. They wouldn't have come to the hospital unless they had collapsed because they didn't have money or time for any medical treatment. I had seen too many of such patients since I came here. Whenever possible, I would sneak out of my father's ward and loiter in the corridor or go to the vestibule at the front entrance, where I would draw lines with white chalk on the cement floor and play hopscotch. My solitary fun was frequently interrupted by the rushing in of panicked peasants who carried homemade stretchers or planks on which lay motionless bodies covered with quilts of different colors—white, blue, pink, red—with traditional floral patterns of peonies and lotus. The carriers would dash directly toward the emergency room on the right side of the entrance, but they were always intercepted by white-gowned nurses who ordered them with stern and frosty faces to stay in the corridor and wait. Sometimes the relatives and friends would start weeping or wailing; others just placed their stretchers on the floor and sank into dull silence.

They would wait alongside of the cold stark corridor wall day after day and night after night. There were not enough wards or beds for every patient who was brought in. Occasionally, nurses in white robes and caps, wearing broad gauze masks, passed by like ghosts. A few times, they affixed an IV line to one or two patients, but most of the time, they simply took a look and left. The sullen and unkempt relatives and fellow villagers would sit at the head or the end of the stretchers with their backs leaning against the wall and their eyes staring vacantly, their faces worn out and downcast.

Some would chat in whispers. Others sat silently dozing off. Still others played poker to kill the time. Every now and then one of those bodies lying beneath its quilt would turn and twist, moaning and murmuring. If they threw up blood, some of the relatives would stop whatever they were doing and rush to the emergency room door, screaming for help; others just stayed put, wiping away blood with yellow straw paper or a piece of old cloth.

Most of these companions were men. Occasionally, there were a few women, older woman in their fifties who sat beside the stretchers of their sons or husbands or brothers, either stitching soles of shoes or sewing clothes. But one time I saw a young woman in her early twenties, wearing a large indigo print triangular head scarf embroidered with a pattern of white lotus. She sat cross-legged on the floor beside a bamboo stretcher, her feet tucked under her legs. She had a half-finished sole of a cloth shoe in her hands and a wicker basket tied with straps on her back. At first, I didn't pay much attention to what was inside that basket, but I noticed that every now and then she would turn her head around and hum a soft and sugary tune to its contents. Then I saw a baby sound asleep in it. As she gently rocked the basket back and forth, her eyes focused all the time on the body lying on the stretcher underneath a quilt with a similar pattern to that of her scarf—white lotus printed on blue cloth. Once in a while, the body would start shaking with violent coughs and then spit blood over the quilt. The young woman would put down her sewing, lift a corner of her head scarf, and gently wipe the blood off that half-covered face. When the body calmed down, she would resume her sewing, while humming her sweet tune to the baby and to the man resting under that blue water where lotuses floated in full bloom.

Such a calm and quiet scene was rare, though. Some patients and their companions who lined up along both sides of the wall and waited for the faintest possibility that they would be admitted into a ward or be given a bed, would frequently burst into anger. Their curses coupled with suppressed sobbing and groaning hovered throughout the corridor like wandering ghosts trying to find a resting place. To escape this angry and anguished screaming and crying, I would quickly return to my father's sickroom, which he shared with two other patients whom I called Uncle Chen and Uncle Zhao. The room was rather crowded, with three single beds and three small nightstands, one beside each bed. On each night stand were various medicine bottles and a white enamel mug bearing the red seal of the hospital, Chaohu Area TB Hospital. Most of the mugs' white enamel surface had chipped off, revealing the black rusty metal beneath. The patients often mistakenly used one another's mugs since they all looked so similar. "It won't matter with us sick old men." Uncle Zhao often joked. "We are all the dying fish caught in the same net. Not much time for us to jump out of the boat. But you, my little angel," he waved his right hand toward me, grinning: "You can't ever touch them. I know you had it before. Your baba said you were very brave. Well, you never know. Just be careful, OK? OK now, do you want me to show you how to make a palace lantern?"

At these words I always jumped with excitement and responded at the top of my voice, "Yes, yes, of course!"

That was one of the rare moments of fun within this isolated hospital life. Uncle Zhao had been a photographer for a local newspaper. He had collected many unused pieces of film, transparent and light blue. Using scissors and small carving knives, he cut these film pieces, each about the size of a magazine cover, into different shapes and inserted them into one another at different angles to make a three-dimensional rectangular palace lantern. My father told me it was the special kind of lantern that often hung at the entrance of the royal palace, to scare away the ghosts as well as to illuminate the steps.

I first watched and later helped Uncle Zhao make those palace lanterns. He told me that with the film he had, we could make six lanterns and then we would hang all of them on the rod of the window curtain. Six was a lucky and promising number that would bless us with the things we wished for. Four lanterns were now strung on a rope and swaying in the window; the remaining two were still waiting to be born out of those fragments of blue film that were scattered here and there on Uncle Zhao's bed and night table.

They had been lying untouched since the previous day's afternoon when, just around mealtime, Uncle Zhao was rushed to the emergency room after vomiting a large amount of blood. Later that afternoon, two nurses came to our ward to get his clothing left on the shelf of the headboard of his bed. They rolled up and took away the white sheet, quilt, and two pillows. One of the nurses picked up Uncle Zhao's mug from his night stand, looked at it for a few seconds, and threw it into the waste basket at the corner. They did all this with a dreadful silence that filled the whole room. My father and I sat on the edge of our bed; Uncle Chen sat on his, like three statues. Other than an overhead fluorescent tube blinking with a faint ping-ping sound, the room was so quiet that we could hear each other's breathing.

The window was open, letting in some breeze that sent the four blue lanterns gently swinging. Then I heard one of the nurses ask, "What are these?" She looked at the blue film that was scattered on Uncle Zhao's night stand. "Anyone want to keep them?" I went over and picked up all of the film pieces and placed them on my father's bed. "I will take care of them and will return them to Uncle Zhao when he is back," I muttered, a little nervous fearing that the nurse would deny my request.

She didn't. Instead, she patted me gently on my head, let out a sigh, handed over all the pieces to me and quickly left the room. The breeze for the moment stopped. The air again became thick and sticky. My father and Uncle Chen continued sitting still on their own beds. From our window, I could see the dusty road winding its way into the gathering dusk. It was already our usual walk time. I asked father if he still wanted to go out. His body suddenly jerked as if he had just awakened from a dream. He was often lost like this. I was used to seeing him drift away and then trying to pull himself back from wherever he was. "Yes, yes," he repeated. "Out,

out," but didn't move. I pulled him up and hand-in-hand we passed through the corridor, out of the back entrance, and into the dry and dusty wilderness.

It seemed now to be more difficult to drag my father back to the hospital. He was lost in that silent and mysterious conversation with the solitary house at the other end of the road. The sun went further down and the twilight was darkening. I was getting more and more anxious and even fearful. Picking up his crutches, I patted his back and asked him in a whisper, "Can we go back now, baba?"

At first, he didn't even move, as if my words had been blown away with the dust. So I raised my voice, trying to catch his attention.

"Baba, we have to go now. It's getting dark. See, the sun is almost down."

At this, my father turned around, slowly and painfully, as if he had suddenly grown ten years older in those silent moments.

"The sun is going down, you say?" He then paused for a while, his eyes squinting toward the now dark red horizon and his face wrinkling into a faint smile. Slowly, he turned toward me, and held my hands in his.

"Sanzi, do you want to know what that house is for?"

I turned my eyes away from him toward that silent gloomy figure that seemed to be straining and listening to our conversation.

"No, and I don't want to know, baba. Let's go back." I held his hands tightly and tried to pull him around. But his body seemed to be frozen. Only his voice was floating through the dusky and dusty air.

"It is called taipingfang, a house of peace. The house where the dead stay temporarily before they are buried. That is why it doesn't have windows. Dead people don't need them."

His voice was cut short by a spasm of coughing. And I saw blood. On a white handkerchief. A red circle, like a red moon hanging in a pale sky.

"Do you know where Uncle Zhao went? He is lying inside right now until his relatives take him away."

The red moon, the setting sun, the blood, the body floating in the lidless coffin on the surging red wave.

"I am going there soon. One of these days. Real soon."

He closed his eyes. A solitary tear leaked from beneath the closed lids of his eyes. The corner of his mouth twitched into a bitter smile.

I looked beyond my father toward the dark orange skyline and then at the blurring shadow of the hospital.

I saw the white lotus swim on the surface of deep blue water and the blue palace lanterns swing in the glowing twilight.

I heard the young woman in the indigo triangular head scarf singing to her baby and her man, and I heard Uncle Zhao laughing.

Then I watched the red moon slowly rise from the white hand-kerchief, flying upward through the darkening twilight, toward the orange skyline where it merged with the setting sun. Together with the setting sun, it threw off a light over the dried yellow earth and illuminated it with a warm silvery wash.

A few evening stars bloomed around the moon; one of them flew directly toward me, its wings flashing as it made its way through the dense air and its voice splashing over the dusty river, resonating in the wilderness:

"No, baba, you are not going anywhere. You are staying with me. You are staying here. I won't let you go. I won't!"

My father sat up and listened, and I listened, too. We looked into each other's eyes in silence, as if both were afraid of breaking the spell of that star, that flash, and that voice.

"No, baba, you are not going anywhere. You are staying with me."

Many years later, I can still hear the echo of that voice. I can still see how my father struggled to stand up on his feet, picked up his crutches, and then reached out his hands toward mine. Neither of us said anything afterward. And nothing needed to be said. Side-by-side my father and I turned around and moved forward, leaving behind us the silent dusty river, never once looking back.

As we walked in the sunset's final glow, the twilight deepened into shadows, and more evening stars bloomed. We listened to the stars singing in the tender twilight, knowing that the fading light of the day is always followed by another sunrise.

槐花 **12**

Beyond Darkness

When I opened my sleepless eyes at the dawn of the first day of June 1969, I found myself drowning in a dark cave flooded with bone-chilling water. I was sinking, inch by inch, toward the bottom until finally the only part of my body above the water was my eyes, with which I searched around, panicked but persistent, through the freezing darkness.

It was all dark, below, above, and all around me. My eyes, sour and aching from straining too hard for too long, began losing focus. I saw stars, numerous tiny shapeless stars, swirling and whirling, like fireflies, slicing back and forth through the darkness, scribbling on the vast blackness some mysterious hieroglyphs glimmering in the cold night.

Then my eyes caught a glimpse of a blurring cluster of blue and white looming in the distance. I stared at the cluster for a moment and recognized that it was the butterfly bows on my two plaits. My grandmother used to say that butterflies would bring good luck. Whenever she braided our hair, my sisters' and mine, she always tied big bows with bright-colored ribbons at the ends. "They make you girls look like little butterflies," my grandmother said.

But the wings of the butterflies were now broken. Like me, they were now floating in a circle of the water, unable to go forward or backward. Their blue and white wings were drooping over the surface of the dark water like a pair of hollow eyes, looking languidly into mine.

175

It started raining. Cold hard raindrops fell with a steady beat into the water, small circles rippling out and quivering away in the dark.

Then I heard a sigh, a long and deep sigh hovering in the cave, interrupting the rhythm of rain with its unspeakable sadness and heaviness.

I was startled, my eyes and ears wide open, my heart and mind alert. I thought I knew that voice.

Nainai?

The thick and silent darkness was watching and listening to me.

Nainai?

I waited.

Slowly and soundlessly, a shadow pushed through a now gray curtain of rain. It was an elderly woman. She was standing still, looking straight ahead, now bending over, now straightening up as if she were looking for something she had lost in the dark.

I knew it was she, my nainai, my dear grandma. But how different she looked. Her black and shining hair, which was always rolled into a perfect bun and fastened with a hairpin inlaid with glistening light green jade beads and an ivory comb, was now disheveled like pieces of torn and ragged cloth hanging on her shoulders. Instead of her favorite outfit, a light blue dajing shirt, with a left-side opening in the shape of a crescent moon, she wore a colorless plastic raincoat that shrouded her entire body.

Is that you, grandma?

Silence.

Are you looking for something? Grandma?

Silence.

Why are you alone? Where is my grandfather?

Silence.

Are you crying, grandma?

Silence.

Unbreakable, unspeakable silence.

Then, slowly and silently, the shadow limped away, staggering back into the gray sheet of rain. I wanted to run after her, but my frozen body and crying heart prevented me from seeing her or hearing her any longer.

All I could do was to keep my eyes open, waiting to see that familiar, but chillingly distant, shadow again.
  I was left alone in the dark cave, crying and waiting.

Whenever she mentioned that first day of June, my mother would shake her head as if still in disbelief. *I called you three times, three times. You just wouldn't wake up. It was the Children's Festival. You were supposed to have the swearing-in ceremony. Remember? We were all so worried, your sisters and I. It was just not like you at all. You were crying; your hands and forehead were cold like you had just come out of some ice-house. It was such a warm day. You remember? The first day of June.*

Yes, I remember. That beautiful, sunny morning of the first day of June 1969.

I remember seeing, on waking up, the dazzling June sunlight stream through the wooden window lattice and its sparkling waves dance on the cold cement floor.

I remember hearing myself sobbing, a mist of tears welling up in my eyes through which I saw sunlight turning into a watery rain-bow. At the other end of the rainbow was that lonely and lingering shadow whose whisper was still hovering in my ears long after that deafening silence.

But the shadow disappeared and the sound was lost. I was left alone, sitting in bed, staring through the misty rainbow, wondering what my dear grandma was searching for in that dark and damp cave.

That was to be a special day for me, the day I was to be sworn in as a new member of Little Red Guard, a revolutionary organization for elementary school students. For me it was one of the few hard-won opportunities that I hoped could help my family, especially my father. Since 1968, two years after the Cultural Revolution broke out, my father had been in a labor camp where he, like many other intellectu-als, engaged in a heavy physical labor, working like a beast of burden, pulling plows through the fields, hoeing soybean seedlings, planting rice shoots, cleaning latrines and pigsties, carrying manure to the field, making sun-dried mud bricks for building houses, until one day he fell onto the ground while carrying two baskets of bricks on a shoulder pole. His lower back was twisted, causing an excruciating pain that soon spread from the back down to his legs.

From the time he was sent back home on a stretcher, he had never been able to walk on his own. Bedridden most of the time, he was still given an order that whenever he could walk, he must go back to the camp. Instead of bringing the joy we had expected, my father's homecoming deepened an already dark cloud which, pressing heavily overhead, reminded us all the time of our responsibility as children to do everything we could to lessen this dark cloud by adding some red color to it—the color of revolution and loyalty.

Becoming a member of the Little Red Guard was one of my ways to add some red color to my family. To be admitted, one had to go through a special ceremony which was usually held every first day of June, at the International Children's Festival; it was no exception on that first day of June 1969.

Later that morning, dressed in white long-sleeved shirts and blue pants, boys and girls alike, we marched in two lines led by our teachers towards the only park in the city. In the center of the park was a tract of grassland, at one end of which stood a square wooden stage where the ceremony would be held. First we listened to a few veterans, Red Army and Anti-Japanese war heroes, giving us a speech and cautioning us against forgetting the past, urging us always to be grateful for the good days we were having now. When they finished, all the new members went up to the stage and lined up in front of a red flag, raising our right arms and pledging our commitment to the Communist cause. Afterward, teachers began distributing our certificates to us—red square plastic badges on which were the three golden characters Little Red Guard, supposedly handwritten by Chairman Mao. We pinned them on the upper left side of our chests—a symbol of our loyalty to the Party and our Great Leader.

By the time we were finally free to play, it was approaching noon. The sun was burning like a fireball, scorching the grass into a dry yellow. Tired of standing and sweating in the sun, several of us girls gathered under a gigantic leafy tree nearby, seeking cool air under its shade. Our Chinese teacher, a soft-spoken woman in her late twenties, pointed to the tree and told us that it was a silver apricot tree, about three hundred years old. It still stood tall and straight, with its long and thick branches stretching far up into the cloudless blue sky. "Look at these leaves," The teacher pointed to the deep green fan-shaped leaves rippling slightly in the breeze. "They are one of the indispensable ingredients in many herbal medicines." While we listened, one of the girls plucked a leaf from one of the branches and waved it at us. "I need a fan to cool me off." she joked. With nothing better to do, we all reached for our own leaves.

Before the teacher noticed, it was a little too late. All of us had at least a couple of leaves in our hands.

"What are you doing? Don't pick the leaves! Never pick leaves from a silver apricot tree! Bad, bad luck! Don't you know that?"

The teacher, always poised in her temper and in her voice, was now screaming and frantically shaking her hands as if she wanted to fan away some invisible presence.

We all recoiled. I looked down at my palms. Two blades of green leaves stared at me with a frosty coldness. I shuddered. A gust of grisly wind blew up my back and stayed there, shooting a chill right through my spine.

That chill followed me all the way toward home, leaving me shivering in the full blaze of June sunlight.

And home was no longer a comfort either.

It was dark, no light. The stove was cold, no food. The air was stagnant, no movement. The house was shrouded by a deadly silence that was now and then broken into pieces by a muffled sound of weeping.

That was my mother.

My head felt dizzy and my legs started shaking. The square red badge pinned on my chest now seemed to stick through my white shirt, slowly piercing a hole deep into my flesh.

My father was sitting at the big square dinner table in the living room, his right hand covering his eyes and his left holding his crutches.

Your grandfather just passed away this morning.

Father's words blurted out, his voice choked with a suppressed sob, tears breaking through his fingers and sliding down his cheeks.

And then I saw my two older sisters, both with red and swollen eyes, packing.

Your mother and I have to leave right away to get your grandma, my father said.

Two weeks later, my parents returned and with them, my grandmother.

It was a mid-June afternoon. The sun was still hanging over the edge of a scarlet sky, exhaling a burning breath. The air was thick with a sweltering heat. Not far away from the sun, a half-moon quietly climbed up, its translucent and watery beams flowing over golden-red clouds. Scattered here and there around the moon were several evening stars, twinkling with a blue and orange hue.

My sisters, brother, and I, all wearing shorts and shirts, sat on the cement stairs in front of our front door watching the setting sun, the moon and the stars, breathing through the dense air, and waiting quietly and patiently for the arrival of our grandmother and our parents. Four pairs of eyes all focused on a narrow stone path that started from the stairs and wound into the distance, like a small creek flowing in the warmth of the setting sun, reflecting on its surface the light of the moon and the stars.

And then, on this silent waterway, there appeared three shadows, equally silent and soundless, floating toward us.

Our grandmother, supported on each side by our parents, inched up the narrow stone stream in slow and unsteady steps. For a moment, none of us could move, as if our legs were held back by some unseen ghosts. Was this the same old grandma who had just left us two months before? She seemed shrunken, her blue dajing shirt flapping over her now smaller and frail body. Her forehead, before so smooth and shining but now darkened with deep long wrinkles. Her velvet black bun was only a knot of gray ashes.

As my grandma trudged painfully toward us on her bound feet with help from my parents, we could see that she was visibly shaking as if with a terrible cold and a high fever. Smiling at us, she murmured something incoherent. Her eyes looked first at us, then through, and finally beyond. Like the moon and the stars, she was so close, and yet so far away. Her body was an elusive shadow that we couldn't embrace, a shadow that was falling like an autumn leaf in slow and lingering descent, a shadow that reminded me of that beautiful June morning when I found myself trapped in that dark and dreadful cave, crying and struggling to find a way out, for my grandma and for myself.

After their return from my grandparents' city, my parents never once talked about my grandfather's death. We never asked and thus never knew exactly how my grandfather died so suddenly. His death, along with its secret, like a stone, was tossed ruthlessly by an invisible hand into a deep pond and quickly sank to the bottom and lay there beyond anyone's touch.

One thing I did know and saw every day was that my grandma seemed to be slipping farther and farther from us into a silent land.

Ever since my oldest sister had been born in the mid-1950s, my grandma had left her own home and moved in with my mother, who was only twenty-one at the time, to help her take care of her first-born and then the three children who followed. Long before the Cultural Revolution, my parents, like many other intellectuals, had already been caught up in one political whirlwind after another. While my parents were swept up in the revolutionary windstorm and carried farther and farther away from us, my grandmother, with her delicate shoulders and her three-inch feet, had propped up the falling sky and shielded us from the outside tempests. She put her own life on hold and came to live with us. Every two or three months or so, she would go back to her own home to take care of my grandfather and her two sons for about two weeks, before returning to her four young grandchildren who were like four little birds, craning their necks and eagerly waiting for their dear sweet Nainai to return, to cook and wash for them, to tell them bedtime stories, and to sing lullabies to them.

Once or twice a month, my grandfather, who worked as a chief engineer in a big factory, would come to our place for a visit. Though each visit was short, his laughter and stories stayed with us long after he left. When he was young, my grandfather had once worked as an apprentice in carpentry. He still kept the hobby of woodcarving. Each time he visited, he would bring various kinds of wooden artifacts for everyone. Just as he loved the craft of carpentry, he also loved telling stories, which might explain why there was such a deep bond between father and the son-in-law. Like my father, my grandfather seemed to have endless stories to tell, stories about himself and those he knew, stories about wars, about his flour mill and about how he started out with his bare hands and became an accomplished entrepreneur and later, a chief engineer. He and my father would spend hours and hours chatting and conversing. Whenever grandfather told stories, my father always listened attentively, smiling and laughing with him. Often we didn't quite know what they were laughing about, but just to hear the laughter in our house again was such a reassurance to our young minds.

But after the summer of 1968, his visits became less and less frequent. Several times after I had gone to bed, I overheard my grandmother and my mother whispering and weeping. Each time my grandmother went back to my grandfather's, she stayed longer and longer. Although worried, we always waited patiently for her to return.

When she did return to us, two weeks after the first day of that June, my grandmother was a changed person. She was still the same granny who took care of us, cooking dinner, washing clothes, and doing other household chores. But the sweet musical rhythm that always accompanied everything she did was gone. Sometimes she moved around, slowly and hesitantly, like a sleepwalker who wasn't sure what to do or where to go. She still tucked us in, telling us bed-time stories, sometimes even singing a few folk tunes, but her voice sounded tired and often shook; she still combed and braided our hair, but often she would forget to tie ribbon bows at the end of our plaits. Many nights I woke up and saw her through thick cotton mosquito netting, sitting on the edge of our big wooden bed, with her arms hugging her shoulders, rocking back and forth silently. Occasionally, she let out a deep and heavy sigh that made my heart weep, just as it had in that frightening dream on that beautiful morning of the first day of June.

Fifteen years after that June morning, on another dawn in the early spring of 1985, my grandmother passed away at the age of seventy-eight, having taken care of us four children and watching us grow up and leave home one by one. She had been sick and almost completely bedridden for a long time. The day before she died, she told my mother that she was cold and wished to go outside to warm herself in the sun. It was still very chilly in the early March, although the sun was becoming warmer each day. My mother sat her in a bamboo chair padded with a light blue cotton quilt, and placed the chair near one of the living room windows facing south. It was noon. The early spring sun shone through the glass and onto her motionless body. She sat quietly, smiling while dozing off and falling asleep—a sleep she never awoke from.

I remember that early spring morning when I was sitting on a wooden chair in a classroom as a graduate student at Shandong University in the north, listening to our American professor chant poems from Walt Whitman's "Song of Myself." His deep voice echoed in the classroom suffused with pleasant and comforting spring sunlight.

> *I believe a leaf of grass is no less than*
> *The journey-work of the stars.*

Then we heard a knock at the door. Before the professor answered, the door was pushed open and standing there was the

Party Secretary of the Department, a stern-faced woman who waved her right hand at me, "Your call." She raised her voice, while the rest of class suddenly became quiet. I tiptoed out of the classroom, closed the door behind me, and followed her through the dim hallway toward her office at the other end of the building.

The call was from my mother. She told me that my grandmother had passed away and that she and my father had already made funeral arrangements. She didn't want me to come back home, since school had just begun. She sounded exhausted, her voice barely audible at the other end of the line. I couldn't hear my own voice, either.

Slowly placing the receiver back on the hook, I turned around and staggered out of the office back into the dim hallway. Finally reaching the classroom and opening the door, I paused. The sunlight flooded toward my face and for a moment, I couldn't see anything. A familiar mist of cold tears blurred my vision and I saw, again, that watery rainbow, although this time, I couldn't see anything or anybody at the other end.

Later that afternoon, in the warm glow of darkening twilight, I went to the forest of silver birches at the west side of our campus. The sunlight slanted through the trees and the rain from the previous night flickered on bare branches. I loved these birches for their straight, graceful trunks, for their deep and watchful eyes that could touch one's heart with a tender sweetness. My father once told me that birches didn't have those human eyes for nothing. "If you ever need to, go and talk to these birches," he said. "They will listen, with both eyes and hearts wide open."

Now standing in front of these thoughtful, often tearful, eyes, I wondered what they would say to me or I to them.

There appeared on the tree branches a few buds showing a tender green and beside the trees tiny leaves of grass were swaying nervously yet excitedly in the gentle spring breeze. I bent over and ran my fingers through the soft grass. One tiny, tear-shaped blade got stuck on my right palm, and then, out of nowhere, I heard again that fear-ridden voice of my Chinese teacher echoing through the forest: "Don't pick the leaves! Bad, bad luck!"

I shuddered, and silence descended like the gathering dusk.

I rubbed my palms and let the blade fall through my fingers. Then I touched the cracked bark of the birches, trying to wipe away tears from their dry and wrinkled eyes, but could no longer hold back my own.

How does that matter? Luck or no luck? Does it have anything to do with luck at all?

Where is my grandmother now? Is she with my grandfather? And where is he? What was she looking for in that dark cave? What was she trying to say to me? What had happened to my grandmother on the morning of June 1st, 1969? What had happened to us these past twenty years? "The Song of Myself," "Leaves of Grass." What do they mean to us?

These questions haunted me long after that beautiful but frightening morning in June. Years after my grandma was gone my parents still kept silent about my grandfather's death. Grown-ups by then, my siblings and I were as much in the dark as when we were younger. The passage to the bottom of that pond seemed forever sealed and the stone remained unfathomable, until my father finally told the story in the form of an essay that was published in a literary journal in the late summer of 1986, seventeen years after we first learned about our grandfather's mysterious death.

That was how I finally got hold of the truth of what had happened to my grandfather, along with many other friends and strangers. My father never explained to us why he didn't tell us first before telling the public. And I wondered if he could have told us even if he had wanted to. Writing perhaps helped him avert a tormenting reality of having to confront his children and to answer questions he might never be able to answer. Although the bleak reality was not necessarily softened by written memories, the screen of memory could indeed filter out some of the harshest details.

Nevertheless, the memory, frozen into the matrix of written words, turns into a silent monument which, like those watchful eyes of the silver birches, has found its way deep into my heart and stayed.

In the spring of 1969, the third year into the Cultural Revolution, my grandfather was dismissed from his position as chief engineer at the Air Pressure Machine factory. His history of once owning a flour mill put him in the category of the "exploiting class" and thus the people's enemy. Frequently, he was forced to attend denunciation meetings which centered on one theme—he had to do endless self-criticism and to beg for forgiveness for his "exploitation" and "oppression" of workers.

After one of those denunciation meetings, my grandfather didn't return home. There was no sign of him as late afternoon turned into evening, and evening into night. My grandma thought he might have dropped by some of his friends' and spent the night there.

What she didn't know, of course, was that my grandfather had never left the factory after the meeting. Later that evening, somebody saw him sitting on the edge of a well in the garden in front of his office building. They exchanged a few words, and he asked my grandfather why he did not go home. My grandpa replied that he wanted to rest for a while and that he would leave soon.

But he never did.

At dawn on June 1st, 1969, my grandfather's body, swollen and smeared with mud, was found floating on the surface of the water in that deep and dark well.

If my heart had ached whenever I wondered about my grandfather's sudden death, it started bleeding each time I thought of his way of dying. I couldn't imagine how my grandfather, who was about six feet tall, with strong and broad shoulders and an even stronger and broader spirit, could be trapped within that dark narrow space. If it had been a river, he at least could have stretched himself out. If he changed his mind at the last minute, he could have swum back to the shore—he was a good swimmer. But this was no river with a shore. In the well there was no other way out; there it was too dark for him to see beyond.

He must have sat beside that well for the whole night, with darkness looming above, beneath, and around him, darkness looming in his mind and heart. Darkness was what my grandfather saw in his last moment.

That was the moment in which I was trapped when I was lost in that horrifying dream, in which I watched in despair while my grandma disappeared into the silent darkness. Although the shadow cannot be seen and no sound is heard, that moment stays with me. It gleams like a clear full moon hanging over a black forest; it sings like a clear-bottomed river flowing through a blue grassland. I see my reflection in the glow of the moon and hear my voice in the song of the river.

But the reflection and the voice are not mine alone.

Whenever I open my eyes to the sparkling waves of the June sunlight, I can see many shadows the sun has cast behind. Through a mist of tears I watch those shadows ride on the arc of the rainbow, flying out of the darkness.

Epilogue

Once upon a time, there is a mountain.

In the mountain, there is a temple.

In the temple, there is an old monk who lives with a young monk.

One day, the old monk begins telling stories to the young monk.

He starts: "Once upon a time, there is a mountain, and in the mountain, there is a temple, and in the temple, there is an old monk who lives with a young monk . . ."

". . . who is going to tell a different story."

The young monk continues.

The old monk smiles and says, "I know you will. Go ahead. I will listen."

The young monk then begins: "Once upon a time . . ."

His voice flies across the green ocean of pine forest. The flash of its wings matches the clear blue sky and the echo of its singing sweeps upward from the valley of the mountain.

The curtain of night falls. The moon rises. The evening stars bloom.

Tomorrow will be another day of telling.